Seven Years
Campaigning *in the* Peninsula
and the Netherlands

1808 ~ 1815

Seven Years
Campaigning *in the* Peninsula
and the Netherlands
1808 ~ 1815

Volume Two

Sir Richard D. Henegan

NONSUCH

First published 1846
Copyright © in this edition 2005
Nonsuch Publishing Ltd

Nonsuch Publishing Limited
The Mill, Brimscombe Port, Stroud, Gloucestershire, GL5 2QG
www.nonsuch-publishing.com

British Library Cataloguing in Publication Data.
A catalogue record for this book is available from the British Library.

ISBN 1-84588-040-4

Typesetting and origination by Nonsuch Publishing Limited
Printed in Great Britain by Oaklands Book Services Limited

CONTENTS

INTRODUCTION TO THE MODERN EDITION

IN 1807 political and military dominance of Europe was split between two powers. France under Napoleon Bonaparte, having defeated Austria, Prussia and Russia on the battlefield, held sway over the continental mainland; Great Britain, following Horatio Nelson's great victory at Cape Trafalgar in 1805, ruled the waves. Napoleon, under the pretext of preparing to invade Portugal, effectively occupied Spain, and, in April 1808, deposed the king and placed his own brother, Joseph, on the throne. The Spanish rose up in revolt against this outrage and the British found a new ally in the Peninsula.

A British expeditionary force landed in Portugal in August 1808. Sir Richard D. Henegan, as Military Commissary in the Field Train, was responsible for the movement of the artillery and ensuring that it was adequately supplied with ammunition. During the later stages of the campaign, from 1813 to 1814, he was Ordnance Commissary in command of the Field Train, charged with providing transport, supplies and equipment for the artillery and the engineers, as well as all the small-arms ammunition for the Anglo-Portuguese army of more than 70,000 men.

This second volume of Henegan's reminiscences covers the latter stages of the campaign in Portugal and Spain, including the aftermath of the Battle of Vittoria[1] and the storming of San Sebastian in 1813. The French army in the Peninsula was finally defeated and the British pursued them over the Pyrenees into France. Napoleon abdicated in April 1814, the Bourbon monarchy was restored to the throne of France and Henegan returned to England, before being ordered to America to fight against the United States in the so-called War of 1812. Before he could set sail, however, Napoleon escaped from his captivity on Elba in March 1815 and Henegan was ordered once more to fight the French. He was sent this time to the Netherlands, under the command of the Duke of Wellington, where he was again in command of the Field Train, and he was present at the battle which would be the Iron Duke's greatest victory and the final defeat of Napoleon: Waterloo.

Seven Years Campaigning in the Peninsula and the Netherlands is written from an unusual perspective, in that Henegan was not involved in the actual fighting, but in supporting those who were. He makes clear what a vital role the artillery and the engineers played in the battles: while they may not have achieved the glory of the infantry and the cavalry, their role was equally vital. It also becomes clear just how important the Field Train was to Wellington's success and what a large and complicated task it was to support an army in the field. His final operation, mopping up the last remnants of Napoleon's army in support of the Prussians under Prince Augustus, involved a 'battering-train' (artillery for siege warfare) of 245 heavy guns and mortars, 288,000 rounds of ammunition and 19,000 barrels of gunpowder, which required 3,000 horses to transport.

Henegan's account of the campaigns in the Iberian Peninsula and the Netherlands is remarkable for the attention its author pays to what happens between the battles. He is particularly interested in the difficulties and dangers faced by the ordinary soldiers, and especially the artillerymen. He is loud in his praise of those whose gallantry was overlooked by those responsible for awarding honours and does not let the reader forget the part played by the Field Train in the campaign. The civilian populations of Portugal, Spain, France and the Netherlands do not escape his notice either, and he is not blind to their good qualities, just as he is vociferous in his condemnation of British troops who engaged in rape and pillage. And he has a very humane attitude to those killed or wounded in the fighting; they are more than mere statistics to him, he sees and is affected by the suffering which conflict causes.

Seven Years Campaigning in the Peninsula and the Netherlands is an engagingly-written narrative of the author's experiences with the Field Train of the British Army during the Napoleonic Wars. Sir Richard D. Henegan gives first-hand accounts of the battles as well as descriptions of the lives of the soldiers and the local people and anecdotes of his own adventures. Informative and involving, it is an important record of the Peninsular War and the Battle of Waterloo.

1. The author uses 'Vittoria,' although the modern spelling is 'Vitoria.'

CHAPTER I

SCENES FROM THE BATTLEFIELD

BY dawn of day, I was at Colonel Dickson's quarters making arrangements for replacing the expenditure of ammunition that had taken place in the battle, both for the troops and brigades of artillery and for the several divisions of the army. This duty completed, I proceeded with a party of the Field Train to the battle plains to ascertain the full amount of guns captured from the enemy; and such was the zealous promptitude with which my department executed the arduous duty of collecting the immense mass of war materiel, that a detailed return of it was given to Lord Wellington before his despatches were written, thus enabling his Lordship to head them with the glorious intelligence of "one hundred and fifty-one pieces of cannon, and four hundred and fifteen waggons of ammunition having remained in the hands of the British army."[1]

The scene of the battlefield, as I traversed it, in the course of my duties, stripped as it then was of all illusive excitement and din of war, produced a train of the most painful reflections. Suffering was there, in all its agonising forms, from the dying wretch, whose expiring groans vibrated on the air, to the wounded soldier, who yet could look around with hope for succour.

Spaniards were there plundering the stranger, whose gallant blood had flowed for the cause of liberty and Spain; and women, if such they could be called, like wolves, were prowling over the field stripping the insensible clay, and sometimes even hastening the spirit from its "dull abode."

Impressed with horror at the sight of so many fiends in female form, I crossed rapidly the field of slaughter, and coming to a remote part of it, beheld a scene that reconciled me to the sex. A woman, young in years, and of a most interesting appearance was seated on the earth, by the side of a shallow grave, that she appeared to have but recently finished. Stretched close beside her, in the cold sleep of death, lay the form of a British soldier, over whom she leant in all the convulsive writhings of genuine grief! On an opposite bank, with eyes deeply and sternly fixed on her, reclined a wounded French grenadier—that man's face has lived in my remembrance; his hard set features expressed the fierce determination to die, rather than to complain. Yet, from the earnestness with which he gazed on the work before him, it was possible, nay probable that some chord of tender remembrance had been struck, some thought of home had subdued the natural sternness of his mind; some regret had followed the sad forebodings of the heart, that his bones, unsepulchred, would whiten on a foreign soil; unblessed, unhallowed by the tear of love.

The grief of the mourner was too sacred for intrusion; my attention therefore turned to the wounded Frenchman; and giving to him a few drops of brandy, which I found in a canteen upon the field, I promised to send him assistance as soon as possible. He scarcely seemed to notice, or to heed my words; but when, on the following day, I visited the hospital into which he had been removed, a look of gratitude beamed from his eye as I approached him.

At no great distance from the group I have described, lay a very youthful French officer, whose ghastly and death-hued countenance bespoke the extent of his sufferings; he had covered himself with a blanket, and at the moment I saw him, a Spaniard, who durst not have met him man to man in the field, was in the act of depriving him of this poor luxury; the youth grasped it with a hand, in which all the strength of his frail existence seemed concentrated, and looked the defiance that he could not breathe; I arrested the Spaniard's arm in the ruthless act; and on the following day, when my duties again called me to the field, I saw the gallant youth stiff and cold, beneath the blanket that I had been means of preserving to him.

In returning that same night to Vittoria, I met General Hay, whose anxiety had brought him from his brigade at Tolosa, where it had been halted, to make some inquiries respecting his son, who had been dangerously wounded by his side in the battle. He had called at almost every house and hospital in the city, without success, and accepted the offer of a bed at my quarters. The following morning, by daylight, the General rose to return to his division, his mind still unrelieved from suspense. In opening the window to order his horse, he saw the serjeant in whose care his son had been left, and eagerly inquired how he was getting on. The serjeant replied that Captain Hay had only just expired, at a house within three doors from that in which his father and myself had passed the previous night. The General was conducted to all that remained of his gallant son, and having given vent for a while to the feelings of a father, those of the soldier returned. Wringing my hand, he mounted his horse, and left Vittoria; to lead his men to future victories, and to meet, a few months afterwards, in an advanced age, the same honourable fate that had cut off his son in the bloom of youth.[2]

1. In the Gazette Extraordinary from Downing Street, dated July 3rd, 1813, it will be seen that this return— signed by the author as Military Commissary of Ordnance, and chief officer of the Field Train—formed a principal feature in the despatches of Lord Wellington; and yet, nearly twenty-five years afterwards, the editor, or rather compiler of the Duke's despatches, thought fit to exclude altogether the name that guaranteed, and was exclusively responsible for the correctness of the information afforded to Lord Wellington.

If truth be the aim and end of history, the author who writes for posterity should substantiate the facts he records, by the authority upon which those facts have become history.

2. This lamented officer was killed on the 14th of April, 1814, at St. Etienne, before Bayonne, gallantly repelling the sortie made by the French from that fortress.

CHAPTER II

THE AFTERMATH OF VITTORIA

MOST great battles are prolific in subjects for after talk, and that of Vittoria was not exempt; for every one had some story to tell of what he had personally seen. I remember having myself witnessed, on that day, an act of humanity, performed by an officer to whom I was sincerely attached; an officer as brave as gentle, and so truly a Christian, that no man had ever heard an oath from his lips, even in those moments of vexed feeling that try the temper most.

Sir Augustus Frazer, of whom I speak, commanded the horse-artillery at Vittoria, he was riding at the head of Major Gardner's troop, along a narrow road, with the guns almost at a gallop; when he saw a wounded French officer lying in the centre of the road. Another minute, and the ponderous weight of the guns would have crushed the sufferer into the earth as they passed over him; but anxiety to save gave Sir Augustus Frazer the strength to do so. With the rapidity of thought he threw himself from his horse, dragged the Frenchman to the bank that skirted the road, and remounting with the same rapidity, had barely time to escape the fearful death from which he had saved an enemy.

During the heat of the action, Deputy Commissary-General Booth, accompanied by Mr. Larpent—who had just been exported from England in the civil capacity of Judge Advocate to the army—most narrowly escaped paying a severe penalty for the curiosity of seeing the fight. These amateurs, both of them very conspicuous—one from the enormous black feather that he wore, and the other from a still more enormous white feather—squatted themselves upon a mound of earth, protected in front by a little thicket of stunted trees, and beyond that by our own troops; here they amused themselves by viewing from a distance the show, doubtless feeling as much personal security as might have been indulged in at a review in Hyde Park The sight of our soldiers in front had banished all thoughts of danger in the rear, from whence, however, a party of French dragoons bore down upon them, attracted by the importance attached to feathers of such long proportions. The Assistant Commissary General was indebted to his feather for his escape, for having left both hat and its appendage in the hands of the dragoon who would have seized him, he managed to slide down the hill into the little thicket beneath, which afforded him a refuge. The Judge Advocate was less fortunate; retaining his magnificent head-gear, he lost his liberty, and was marched off a prisoner in great triumph by the dragoons, who imagined they had effected the capture of a general-officer judging by the length of his feather.[1]

Colonel Burton, of the Welch Fuzileers, had been appointed Commandant of Vittoria, and by the help of the working parties, with which he supplied me, I completed the task of parking the guns and ammunition captured from the French. When this was done, I received orders to transfer them over to the Spanish Governor of Vittoria, and to join the artillery battering train at Passages, where preparations were making for the siege of San Sebastian. During the period of collecting together the war materiel at Vittoria, upwards of one hundred and sixty private carriages were brought into the park. Some of them were fitted up in the most costly manner, with velvet and silk linings, and as they were only incumbrances in the park, and totally useless to the army, I made them over to Colonel Burton, suggesting that they might perhaps be advantageously distributed among those inhabitants of Vittoria, who had suffered from the depredations of the French. He gladly acceded to the proposal, and it was not until after the fall of San Sebastian, that I heard of the large treasures in money and jewels that had been found within the linings, and other parts of the carriages I had so unwittingly disposed of.

There were also discovered, at the same time, some curiosities of the female *boudoir*, so peculiarly ingenious that Sir Colin

Campbell—the permanent Commandant of head-quarters—thought it his duty to hand them over for the inspection of the Commander-in-Chief; where-upon His Excellency, for some mysterious reasons that were not made public, ordered, without loss of time, an escort of the Royal Irish to convey the French ladies to their lords and masters.

Very shortly after the battle of Vittoria there appeared in the artillery orders, promulgated by the Assistant-Adjutant-General—Colonel May—a notification from the Master-General, Lord Mulgrave, that his Royal Highness the Prince Regent had been graciously pleased in consideration of the very striking and unexampled circumstance of the whole of the British artillery having been brought into action at the battle of Vittoria, and the whole of the enemy's artillery having been captured in that glorious victory, to grant to all the officers, entrusted with the command of divisions or brigades, an allowance for good service in the following proportions: to the officers commanding divisions each 10s. per diem; to the officers commanding brigades, each 6s. per diem; and to Colonel Dickson, as commanding officer of the whole, 20s. per diem.

Notwithstanding the high degree of military merit that must always be attached to the names of Robert Gardner, Webber Smith, Hugh Ross, Norman Ramsey, and other officers who commanded as Captains of Artillery on the plains of Vittoria, it may perhaps be asked why the artillery—valuable as were its services—should have been selected for special reward, where each corps vied with each other in conspicuous gallantry. None were more surprised at the circumstances than the fortunate officers who were so selected, but whatever might have been the justice or injustice of thus marking out the officers of artillery for a special sign of approbation from the country, it is undeniable that the Field-Train should have been included in the grant; for the high state of equipment which had "enabled the whole of the British artillery to be brought into action," was essentially contributed to by the able exertions of the department of which I was the chief officer.

It is unnecessary to observe upon the unity that exists between a soldier and his means of warfare, without the efficiency of which, his exertions are paralysed; and in that same close connexion did the Field-Train stand united to the Royal Artillery.

The following opinion on this subject was given by Lieutenant-General Sir Julius Hartman K.C.B., of the German artillery—than whom no officer is possessed of greater experience in the military profession. "The artillery to be well and efficiently served, must have an active and well organized Field-Train department. It is a branch of the same tree; the honour won by the former must redound to the latter; and, therefore, in my opinion, rewards and remunerations should be equally shared."

Many accidents took place on the field of Vittoria, owing to the immense quantities of ammunition that lay scattered over its extent. The Spaniards, in their search for booty, opened several tumbrils, in the hope of finding concealed treasure, and careless of the sparks that dropped from their inseparable companion, the cigar, often occasioned an explosion, of which they were themselves the victims.

Upon one occasion, a catastrophe was averted by the presence of mind of an officer of the Field-Train on duty, which in its effects would have blown up the whole city of Vittoria. A tumbril containing live shells was discovered to be on fire in the midst of the captured park of ammunition. There was a moment's hesitation; for fearful was the alternative by which alone could be saved the number of human beings within reach of the terrific explosion that must inevitably follow the ignition of the shells. An immense mass of combustible matter lay loosely scattered around, and upwards of one hundred thousand pounds of powder. The loss of another moment would have been fatal, when the officer above mentioned sprung into the burning tumbril, and having thrown out the live shells beyond the reach of the fire, took in his arms the last—of which the fuse was already ignited—and carrying it thus to an adjacent deep ditch, rolled it to the bottom, where it exploded harmlessly.[2]

It has often been my lot to witness the beneficial results of presence of mind, and also the lamentable results produced by the want of this valuable quality and essential attribute even to valour. Many bold hearts, who have been fore-most in the path of danger, have fallen victims to causes that required but a small portion of energies they possessed to have averted; but so is man constituted, that too frequently according to the cry of fear, or of triumph, that re-echoes around him, so are his physical and moral energies paralysed or drawn forth; and it is as true, that the stoutest hearts have been known, in cases of sudden surprise, to respond to the craven who first gave the signal of alarm, as it is, that dispositions, naturally weak and cowardly, have been rallied into daring achievements, by the presence and co-operation of the brave.

On the evening that preceded my departure from Vittoria, I went to say farewell to my fellow-lodger, the French Colonel, who had been gradually progressing towards recovery since the amputation of his leg. I had visited him almost every day, and the acquaintance between his little boy and myself had ripened into something very like affection on both sides. At parting, the Colonel pressed my hand with kindly warmth, expressing the hope that we might meet again as friends. Madame almost forgot her affectation when thanking me for my attentions to her gallant Lord; and my little friend roared fairly out, when I bestowed a last kiss on his cheek. And so we parted, who a few days before would have cut and hacked at each other, with all the animosity of fighting dogs, at the word of command.

In passing along the corridor, more than half subdued into the melting mood, I saw the light and graceful form of Donna Flora, our fair young hostess, waiting at the end of it as if to speak to me. It is unnecessary to say that I had improved to the utmost of my power my first acquaintance with this fair young being, that had commenced on the first night of my arrival in the apartment of the wounded Colonel. I had also been the happy means of saving her from insult and violence, when an attack was made on her brother's house by his fellow-countrymen, under the impression that he was sold, as they termed it, to the French interests; for such was the position of Vittoria, that although its inhabitants had appeared more than reconciled to the French yoke during the time they were in possession of the town, no sooner were they succeeded by the English, than a counter-revolution of feeling took place, and all those who were even suspected of favouring the French, were violently assaulted in their own houses, and many were even murdered by the excited populace.

As Donna Flora saw me approach, she put her finger to her lips as if to impose silence, and beckoning me on, I followed her into a little room, where two Spaniards were seated wrapt in their large cloaks. No sooner was the door closed, than the girl threw herself at my feet, and with passionate vehemence, declared she would not rise until I had promised to comply with her request, whatever it might be. I confess that I was sorely puzzled; for at that particular time, party spirit ran so high that I feared lest her demand might comprise more than it was in my power to concede. While still hesitating how to compromise matters with the fair petitioner, I found my difficulty's considerably increased by a new supplicant. One of the Spaniards, whose large *sombrero* only left enough of his countenance visible to show its extreme youthfulness, at this crisis, joined his urgent entreaties to Donna Flora's, and thus hemmed in between beauty and distress, I found no other means than to surrender.

The outer works once gained, the other Spaniard who had sat apparently unmoved, and indifferent to the success of the supplicants, now rose, and with the ease and dignity that distinguishes, in most cases, the noble Hidalgo, introduced himself to me as Don Miguel Malafra; one, who had, alas, for Spanish patriotism given such proof of submission to the yoke of France, as to accept the office of a Prefect under that Government. The newly aroused vengeance of his countrymen against all Spaniards so situated had left him but one alternative—escape; and Donna Flora, his near relative, with all the wit of woman, when closely pressed for systematic stratagem, had not scrupled to name me as one likely to aid and abet in the enterprise. The plan that my acquiescence was to mature, was, that the Conde should assume the disguise of a muleteer in my service, and by this means traverse Spain, now to him a hostile country, and seek protection from the French Government. The whole difficulty of the case as regarded the compromise of a British officer's position, rushed at once to my mind; and yet, as so many Spaniards of rank had been in the same renegade phalanx with the Conde de Malafra, without incurring punishment, I could not but think it hard that he should be singled out—the victim perhaps of vindictiveness more than of justice.

Notwithstanding my promise, however, hesitation got the upper hand. I remained silent, and the result might have been very different, had not the younger Spaniard, who saw my embarrassment, removed from a very fair brow the large *sombrero*, and turning to me a pair of dark eyes, almost concealed by a profusion of clustering curls, implored me in the name of woman to save her husband.

When the citadel is carried, it is useless look out for new means of defence, and so in this instance; the heart had given way, and the head was therefore put *hors-de-combat*. I consented to be blown up, if necessary, to show my devotion to the sex, in whose name I had been summoned to surrender, and in half an hour afterwards, the Conde and his fair spouse, Donna Flora and myself sat down to a delightful *petit souper* where we discussed the preliminaries to be observed on the morrow's departure.

The sun was fast sinking in the west on the following evening, when I left Vittoria on my way to Passages. The nature of my situation at head-quarters facilitated the arrangements I had made during the day to insure the safety of Don Miguel and his wife, the latter having also procured the dress of a muleteer to accompany her husband in his flight.

A larger number of mules was allowed to me than to any other officer holding the same rank; and I was, therefore, enabled to send on, in advance, my camp equipage, reserving three mules for my own personal effects, that were to accompany me on the road. A German sergeant who was attached to my party—an upright trustworthy fellow as ever lived—was admitted into the secret, and he managed to load the animals so lightly, as to allow of the additional weight of my noble muleteers.

When all was ready, the Conde and his wife issued from the stable with their respective charges, taking up their position in the rear of my saddle horses. I could not help glancing round to see how the noble lady played her new part, but the dark cloak and slouched *sombrero*, so completely concealed both figure and face, it was impossible to discover the deceit.

Another glance at the lower window of the house we were leaving, showed me Donna Flora kneeling before a little shrine dedicated to the Virgin, praying, as she had promised to do, for the protection of our party.

She turned her beautiful face, bathed in tears towards us, and looked a sad farewell. And thus we parted for ever.

1. Mr. Larpent was sent to Bayonne as prisoner of war, but Lord Wellington, requiring his services as Judge-Advocate, effected his exchange for a French officer of rank.

2. The late Earl of Mulgrave, when Master-General, observed, in allusion to this officer's services, that, "the Board of Ordnance and himself very highly appreciated his conduct and services throughout the war, which they considered entitled him to every encouragement the service could bestow; but, that there existed no precedent to guide the Master-General and Board in granting him any mark of distinction." This remark was made immediately after the unprecedented grant to the officers of artillery at Vittoria.

CHAPTER III

ARRIVAL AT PASSAGES

THE second evening brought us to Villa Franca, where we found Captain Norman Ramsey's troop of horse-artillery, and a brigade of cavalry under General Vandeleur. The former gallant officer was in arrest under circumstances of a peculiar nature. Lord Wellington had met him in the valley of Araquil, on the day succeeding the battle of Vittoria; and had given him orders to put his troop in cantonment in a neighbouring village, and not to move until he received further direction from himself. Early on the following morning, a staff officer, of the cavalry division to which Ramsey was attached, rode to demand the assistance of the troop at the advanced posts. Ramsey explained his position in reference to the orders he had received from Lord Wellington the previous night; but was told that change of circumstances had produced a change of orders, and under this impression, Ramsey led his troop to the advanced post.

With an exuberance of displeasure, Lord Wellington visited this offence, if offence it could be called, totally unmindful of the previous brilliant services of the offender; for Norman Ramsey was one who yielded to none in bravery, talent, and every other quality that constitutes the soldier and the gentleman. The shaft had, however sped, that was to make him a victim; his troop was transferred to the next senior officer, and almost heart-broken at such a sequel to the reputation he had so nobly earned in the many battlefields of the Peninsula, Norman Ramsey was awaiting the mandate that was to send him back to England.

My first object on arriving with my party at Villa Franca, was to obtain some comfortable nook, without creating suspicion, for the night's repose of my muleteers. This was effected by the agency of the German sergeant, who managed to secure to himself the next best quarters to my own. When all was still, he exchanged them for a bed of clean straw in the stables with the mules, and conducted our patrician muleteers to the enjoyment of his own snug roost.

The next morning, I was breakfasting with Norman Ramsey, and the officers of his troop, now commanded by another, when General Vandeleur arrived. Upon entering the room, he went up to Ramsey, and grasping his hand with a brother soldier's warmth, said:

"The object of my visit, Captain Ramsey, is to inspect your troop."

"My troop, General, is mine no longer," answered poor Ramsey, with deep emotion.

"I am glad to say you are mistaken, Captain Ramsey," rejoined the General, "for I am the bearer of orders from head-quarters that authorise me, as I before said, to inspect your troop. The command of it is restored to you."

Ramsey, overcome by his feelings, turned away and wept, while every officer present, and none more cordially than Captain Cater, who had superseded him, gave vent to their joyful feelings at this happy termination; yet, notwithstanding this restoration to favour, the shaft, as before stated, had sped from head-quarters, and Norman Ramsey, whose name had appeared with distinction in the despatches of Vittoria, and who had distinguished himself in every brilliant action in the memorable campaign of 1813, was omitted in the brevet that came out after Vittoria, and left the field at the termination of the war in Spain, without one honorary distinction having been conferred on him.[1]

On leaving Villa Franca, we continued our route to Passages through Tolosa. The road was so unfrequented, that by degrees my companions began to throw off the alarm that they laboured under during the first day's march, and the dark-eyed little Spanish dame would sometimes relax in attention to her sluggish charge, and even ventured to chat with me when I got off my horse to walk by the side of herself or husband.

If a human figure appeared in the distance, the German sergeant gave a preconcerted cough, which was the signal for us all to resume our respective places in the front and rear.

Thus we journied on in safety until we arrived at Passages, where difficulties would have thickened around us, but for the skillful management of our friend the sergeant. My billet at Passages was in an old tumble down house, overlooking the harbour, and as full of long passages, iron gratings, and trap doors, as any locality ever selected by Mrs. Radcliffe for the theatre of her monstrosities. There was an old wooden terrace in front of the house, literally overhanging the ocean, and in the still hour of night, how sweet it was from that old crazy resting place, to view the myriads of stars that lit the southern sky, reflected in their deep bed of azure blue! but dearer even than this to the sentimentalist, were the dark holes and corners that offered security to those who required it.

The ground floor, if such it could be called, once appropriated as store-rooms, but now unoccupied, save by a few articles of old furniture, became the object of our sergeant's speculations, and consequently my quarters. A little kitchen was occupied by the culinary apparatus of my canteens, under the special guidance of José, a Portuguese cook, with so little of good and so much of evil in his composition, that to this day I am inclined to believe that Satan sent him as one of his chef-d'œuvres, to "sink, burn, and destroy" whatever came within his reach on earth. The next chamber was appropriated as my own bed-room, with indeed but scanty furniture, for the whole of my camp equipage, bedding, &c. was transferred to an inner room, in which I had placed Don Miguel and his Donna Margueritta.

The sergeant had exacted, on the part of the refugees, the most complete seclusion in this one apartment and my occupations were of such an out-door nature that but little scope was given for surmise in the old house that we inhabited in common. So things went on, and in the meantime were concluded the operations of disembarking the heavy ordnance and materiel for the Siege of San Sebastian, as well as the equipment of the guns and mortars for the batteries, the whole of which laborious duties devolved upon the department of the Field Train.

Every hour that I could dispose of in the midst of my numerous vocations, was devoted to relieve the monotonous confinement of my Spanish guests; and every evening, after nightfall, found me either listening to the specious reasonings of Don Miguel, in extenuation of his political conduct, or to the soft accompaniment of his lady's guitar, as she sang the deeds of Spanish patriotism or Spanish chivalry.

Alas! that they should live in song alone! The perfume of the flower has been extracted, but the root that bore it is exterminated from the soil.

When danger has surrounded us for a period, without our having sustained any injury, we grow callous to its continuance, in the belief that the security of the past is a guarantee for the future. Sometimes we even forget altogether our position of danger, and advance nearer and nearer with a kind of irresistable fatality, to meet the evil that at first we made so many efforts to avoid. The sequel of my Spanish friend's adventures was an illustration of this truth. In the meantime, I was called upon to quit my quarters in the old crazy house for others in easier communication with those of Sir Thomas Graham and Colonel Dickson. This was the first leak sprung in the bark that I had hoped would have steered my poor refugees safely into port; for although I left them in my old quarters, under the special care of our friend the sergeant, there was another in my establishment, who necessarily had become a sort of demi-confidant; and that other was José.

1. Major Norman Ramsey found a soldier's grave on the plains of Waterloo.

CHAPTER IV

ATTACK ON SAN SEBASTIAN

THE batteries being fully armed, and the magazines formed for supplying them, the artillery under Colonel Dickson opened fire upon the fortress of San Sebastian on the 20th of July.

Our naval force upon the station consisted of only La Surveillante of forty guns, commanded by Sir George Collier, and the Lyra sloop—Captain Bloigh—a force totally inadequate to prevent the garrison from receiving supplies from Bayonne. From the former ship, a party of as gallant fellows as ever lived, was sent on shore to work a battery of six twenty-four pounder carronades, under the command of their first Lieutenant Dowell O'Reilly.

It was the night preceding the attack that I took possession of my new quarters, and anxious, if possible, to transfer Don Miguel and his wife to my new abode, I took a lamp to explore the lower regions of the house, and ascertain its capabilities for my purpose. In descending the stairs, I was greeted with a shout of boisterous mirth, united with the tones of a sharp fiddle; and, following the sounds, I found myself in a large room, appropriated to a grand entertainment.

Tallow candles stuck in bottles, as substitutes for candlesticks, illuminated the fête; large barrels of cider—for the premises were originally intended for this commodity—were unceremoniously stowed away into the corners, to make room for the dancers, with the exception of one, that served as gallery to the orchestra. On it, in triumphal display, stood the scraping fiddler, while upwards of thirty blue jackets were footing the double shuffle of the sailor's hornpipe, till the beams shook and cracked in sympathy.

Along the ceiling ran a double tier of slung hammocks, and this latter circumstance left me in no doubt that these jolly fellows were quartered in the same house as myself. I had scarcely time to give a regret to the annihilation of my plans for the refugees, when the Lieutenant in command stepped up, and giving me Colonel Dickson's compliments, informed me, that by the recommendation of that officer, he had brought his men to my capacious premises. I certainly wished the Colonel in one of the cider barrels for his good counsel, and in one of them he certainly might have been, without receiving any injury, for the blue jackcts had transferred the whole of its contents to the safe keeping of their leathern belts. I was kindly asked to sanction, by my presence, the installation of the sailors into their shore-slung hammocks, and we kept it up merrily until the dawn of that morning, when we commenced our operations against the fortress of San Sebastian. And now having paid due attention to the happy merriment of our Jack tars, let me try to give a faint outline—for description must ever in such cases fall short of reality—of their noble, yet characteristic bearing in the little battery they served.

It was early on the morning succeeding our fun, that I volunteered to show them a short cut to their battery, and headed by the fiddler, who scraped away to the tune of "Jack's alive," we came in sight of the French soldiers upon the ramparts; and much they must have been amused at the sight of the blue jackets cutting capers, and playing every kind of antic that joyous hearts could devise; whilst when a shot boomed over the head of one of the party, the lucky fellow who escaped was made to bend, while his comrades played leap frog over him, and then the never-tired fiddle burst forth with "Jack's alive," or "Hearts of Oak."

The sailor's battery was altogether so gallantly worked, that the artillery and Engineer officers used to drop in by turns, either to say a word of approbation to the men, or to be amused by the original and quaint ways of these amphibious soldiers. Nothing daunted them; nothing put them out, and even if a murderous shell fell, with its levelling vengeance in the little battery, "Jack's

Alive," was instantaneously struck up by the enthusiastic fiddle, to staunch any pang that the loss of one of these gallant fellows, might have inflicted on the rest. Thus three days and nights of incessant firing, on both sides, passed away. On the right of the sailors, was a battery of twenty twenty-four pounders, worked with such skill by the gunners of the Royal Artillery, that the great breach of the fortress was practicable on the evening of the 23rd, a day, alas, that was fraught with direful results to our gallant tars. Up to that time, the casualties throughout the batteries had been comparatively trifling, owing, in a great measure, to their skilful construction by the Engineers, who had afforded all possible protection to the gunners, placing traverses, &c., to save them from splinters of shells, and other accidents.

The French had, in San Sebastian, four immense mortars, from which they threw shells of fourteen inches in diameter—hitherto none of these monsters had found their way to the batteries, but as they passed over our heads, the heavy rush they made through the air, and the terrific noise of their explosion, made us distinctly recognize them, amidst the thundering of all the other guns. The tars had christened them "the babies," and as each "baby," with its own peculiar cry, ranged beyond the mark of their battery, the sailors cut capers at their escape, and the fiddle played.

It was about eleven o'clock on the morning of the 23rd, when one of these awful shells, thrown with fatal precision, appeared in the air, descending like a mighty destroyer, in the direct line of the sailor's battery. The monster alighted on the back of a poor fellow, who had thrown himself on his face as the only chance of escape, and exploding at the same instant, killed, or dreadfully mutilated, seventeen of these noble-spirited champions of England's wooden walls.

The tide of mirth now flowed no longer; the survivors looked at each other in sad astonishment at the sudden thinning of their ranks, and the tones of the scraping fiddle were exchanged for the deep groans of those few in whom life still lingered. There was a boy of the party, who was the beloved of all—handsome, gay, and gallant; and so young, only fifteen, that his messmates would not hear of his accompanying them into the battery, always trying to find for him some duty, that was to detain him within doors; but Ben Harris was not to be kept away from danger; his young heart panted for glory, and he found it, poor little fellow, at a fearful sacrifice. He was found, at a considerable distance, with both his legs blown clean off. I never shall forget the tenderness with which his shipmates carried him into hospital, where he received every care, but the shock was too great for one of his tender years and he survived but a short period.

The good and gallant O'Reilly was blown right through the embrasure, by the rushing whirlwind that accompanied the monstrous shell in its downward flight. Although taken up senseless, he was found to have sustained no serious injury, nor outward wound, yet the early termination of his gallant career at no very long period afterwards, led his friends to believe that he had never recovered from the effects of that concussion. After this disaster, the sailor's battery assumed a completely different aspect; the men worked at their guns with the same activity, but in silence; the merry joke was heard no more, and on revisiting the cider premises that had witnessed the joyous revelling of those whose eyes were now closed in death; I saw that some hand had assigned a humble place against the wall to the now silent fiddle.

CHAPTER V

A FAILED ASSAULT

THE battering train force employed against the fortress of San Sebastian was thus disposed of. On the right of the attack, along the Chofre sand-hills, were twenty twenty-four pounders, four sixty-eight carronades, four ten inch, and six eight inch mortars. On the left, against the fortified convent of San Bartolomeo, were six eighteen pounders, under the direction of Colonel Hartman, of the German artillery. Up the Monte Olia, we had dragged, with great labour, the six eight-inch mortars from the Chofre sand-hills, and from the above eminence we looked into the enemy's batteries of the Mirador, and Monte Orguello.

The several batteries were worked under the directions of Lieutenant-Colonels May and Frazer; Majors Dyer and Webber Smith; and Captains Dubordien, Parker, &c., the whole under the command of Colonel Dickson.

The Engineer department was commanded by Sir Richard Fletcher, ably assisted by Colonel Burgoyne, Majors Ellicombe and Smith, the latter, an officer who had much distinguished himself in the defence of Tarifa, had been selected to draw out the plan of the siege, and to superintend its details.

On the second day of the firing, the artillery lost an officer of great promise in Captain Dubordien, who was killed by the splinter of a shell. On the day of the 23rd, a smaller breach to the right of the main breach was rendered practicable, and preparations were made for the assault before daybreak on the following morning. During the night two thousand men from the fifth division, were placed in readiness in the trenches, but the attack was deferred, in consequence of the conflagration of the houses immediately joining the breach, and during the day of the 24th, the guns from our batteries were employed in destroying the new defences raised by the enemy. In the dead hour of that night, the same party, headed by their gallant leaders, were reassembled in the trenches waiting their signal to advance.

And here it may justly be permitted to remark upon the injudicious arrangements of our first assault on the fortress of San Sebastian. In the first place, the hour elected, was one of complete darkness; a circumstance that carried with it so much of evil, that it ought not to be passed over lightly. Without, for a moment, doubting the innate courage of the British soldier, common sense points out the error of allowing men the power of shirking danger, without being exposed to the wholesome discipline of the eye of comradeship, which alone suffices, in many instances, to make men brave. The same soldiers, who would respond to the cheering cry and bright glance of their officer, under the broad glare of daylight, by rushing to the summit of a breach, might show less enthusiasm in seeking death, if the veil of darkness were to conceal alike their deeds of valour, or the absence of them. In the case in question, the troops had the additional disadvantage of receiving a check to the ardour they at first felt, by the postponement for twenty-four hours of the dangers that threaten, at all times, a storming party, and which certainly did not add to the enthusiasm of the attack.

Long before dawn of day, on the 25th, the storming party issued from the trenches. The leading column was commanded by Major Fraser, of the Royals, headed by the forlorn hope under Lieutenant Campbell, of the 9th regiment, and accompanied by Lieutenant Harry Jones, of the Engineers, who volunteered as guide to the breach. The road from the trenches to the points of attack was bad in the extreme, being upwards of two hundred yards in distance, over sharp pointed rocks, and deep holes of sea-water, that the receding tide of the Arumea river had left.

The Governor of the fortress, General Rey, had not been neglectful of gathering together his powers of destruction against the assailants, and as the latter advanced with as much rapidity as the difficulties of the path would admit, they were exposed to a terrific fire of musketry and shells from the ramparts, while, in front, a heavy discharge of grape showered from the battery of the Mirador, which flanked the approach to the breach. Yet still our men rushed on, headed by their brave officers, whose cheering tones rang audibly through the disordered columns that the narrowness of the uneven road had caused. The forlorn hope made a desperate effort to mount the breach; they partly succeeded, but few survived the attempt, and their gallant leader fell wounded in the fruitless effort to maintain the position. Lieutenant Jones, of the Engineers, was the first to show the way to the summit closely followed by Major Frazer of the Royals, whose loud cry of "Follow me, my lads," was distinctly heard amidst the tumult of the storm, until death froze it on his lips. The foremost men of the Royals pressed closely on, and some few stood by their intrepid officers, but the remainder of the advancing column, awed by the overwhelming fire to which they were exposed on every side, hung back, and turned their muskets upon the enemy on the ramparts. Unsupported by their comrades, the foremost men fell one by one upon the breach, and Lieutenant Jones, misled by the darkness into the belief that his footsteps would be closely followed by the stormers, bravely leaped from the breach into the town below—a distance of upwards of twelve feet. Had his expectations been realized, the fortress of San Sebastian had been our own; but they were not so. And Jones stood alone on hostile ground, a wounded prisoner.

After these discouraging attempts to gain a footing on the breach, it would appear that no combined efforts were made to effect it, yet it was evident from the fate of those gallant fellows who lost their lives on its summit, that such was practicable, and had the noon day's sun shone upon the men at the foot of the breach, there is little doubt but that Lieutenant Jones would have been gloriously followed by a victorious storming party.

The increasing intensity of the enemy's fire raked, with fearful force, our ranks. Darkness still prevailed, each moment added to the confusion, and the stormers, panic-struck at the hot reception they had encountered, endeavoured, amidst the tourbillon of musketry, bursting of shells, and whistling of grape, to regain the trenches. But these were almost as difficult to attain as the summit of the breach. The narrow road stood choked up by the assailants in one dense mass, and it was only when the demon of destruction had fully glutted his appetite, that the diminished numbers of our men opened the means of retreat to the trenches.

The trenches once regained, and the intelligence of our failure promulgated, our batteries reopened a continuous and tremendous fire upon the fortress; the very guns appearing to sympathize in the revenge we were taking for the events of the night.

The grey dawn was just peeping through the eastern sky, and the surrounding objects beginning to emerge from shadowy perceptibilities into the tangibility of their accustomed forms, when Colonel Frazer of the artillery, visited the twenty four-pounder battery, then actively employed against the fortress. His eyes naturally turned in the direction of the scene of the previous night's failure, and through the curling smoke that lightly wreathed through the morning air, he thought he perceived a figure on the summit of the breach. Again it was concealed by the thick flakes of smoke that followed the returning fire of the fortress, and again as the smoke curled off into the blue air, it assumed a more distinct appearance. As the morning's light increased, the outline of the figure became clearly perceptible, and Colonel Frazer could then distinguish that it was a French officer, making sundry telegraphic signals with his sword to the English batteries. The singularity of the circumstance caused Colonel Frazer to stop the firing; which was responded to by a similar cessation from the fortress, and an officer was despatched forthwith for an explanation of this extraordinary proceeding; under the security that was offered by the continuance of the Frenchman's position on the breach, his sword pointed to the earth.

The annals of war present, it is true, many noble actions that proclaim abnegation of self. Many traits of personal heroism, that draw the burst of admiration from our hearts towards the hero, without allowing us time, even had we the inclination to inspect the soundness of the root, of which the action we admire is so beautiful a flower. Perhaps in most cases we might find 'ambition for distinction,' the little bulb from whence great actions spring; but in the present instance, the officer, upon the breach of San Sebastian, risked a thousand times his life in the sacred cause of humanity.

Under the walls of the fortress and strewed along the strand, lay our wounded officers and soldiers. The shells from our batteries bursting over the walls of the fortress, fell upon these poor defenceless creatures, killing and wounding the already wounded, while the shots also rebounded from the walls among them. The spectacle of so much suffering was not to be endured even by their enemies, and a noble spirited young French officer stepping forward to make known their distressing situation, sought the dangerous and conspicuous position on the breach, as the best means to acquaint us with the fatal effect of our own guns on our wounded countrymen.

In consequence of this information, one hour's truce was agreed upon by the belligerents, and a very curious and interesting scene occupied this short period. British and French soldiers were promiscuously engaged in carrying off the sufferers, and it was a subject for reflection to see the ease with which the French soldiers, each encumbered with the burthen of a wounded man, managed to ascend the same breach that that so many had found to be impracticable. It is true that broad daylight was now substituted for the cover of night.

The French made no opposition to the British soldiers taking into their own trenches as many of their countrymen as they could carry off; but those taken by the French in the fortress, became of course prisoners of war. The hour expired, the contending foes returned to their respective strong-holds, the guns recommenced their thundering, and thus may be said to have terminated the first assault on the fortress of San Sebastian. An unsuccessful enterprize, that cost us, in killed and wounded, upwards of five hundred soldiers, and fifty officers; but worse than even the loss of so many gallant fellows were the disheartened, crest-fallen looks that pervaded the ranks of our men, when the full extent of our signal failure was made known. A settled gloom, not unmixed with shame, lowered on every brow, and though unexpressed, there was not one who did not feel how much more might have been done than had been done.

It may easily be imagined that such a feeling in British soldiers rapidly engendered another, that of retrieving the past by a glorious future, and all hearts panted with the one desire to be led a second time against the walls of San Sebastian. In the midst of these aspirations, the movements of the French army caused Lord Wellington to order the whole of the guns, stores, &c., to be sent immediately to Passages for embarkation, and San Sebastian was left in a state of blockade only. The operation of removing the battering train to Passages, and its subsequent embarkation, was effected in all its details by the Field Train department, and I consequently found myself once more located in my crazy quarters overlooking the harbour.

CHAPTER VI

PRESENTIMENTS OF EVIL

MY absence from Passages had cut off all communication between myself and the Spanish refugees, except on two occasions, when that the German sergeant had been over to San Sebastian, to tell me how things were going on with them. From him I learnt that Don Miguel had thrown aside the disguise on which his security depended; and that his frequent absences from home during the hours of evening had destroyed all hopes of his preserving an incognito in the neighbourhood. I heard too that he had quarrelled with my cook, José, and it was with a presentiment of coming evil, that I knocked at the door of his apartment on the first night of my return to Passages. It was opened to me by a lovely woman, in the costume of the Andalusian ladies of rank; nor is it to be wondered at that I started back, unable to trace in the beautiful creature before me any resemblance to the young muleteer I had left in that apartment. I trembled at the change, for I saw broken down at one fell swoop all the benefit that the continuance of our well-conceived plan might have insured; and although, at the first moment, it was exclusively on their own account that I was alarmed, it was impossible for me to conceal from myself that my own position was not slightly embarrassing, in harbouring persons who unequivocally had been employed in the interests of France.

Before I could recover from my surprise, a whistle under the window caused the signora to bound towards the terrace, which led, by a pair of ricketty, wooden stairs, to a little landing-place beneath. Her fair hand threw down a cord, and following her steps, I saw a figure, by the retreating twilight, leap from a small boat, moor it carefully, and in another moment Don Miguel stood before us. To say the truth, we were both embarrassed, though perhaps from different causes, and scarcely could I find patience to listen to his plausible reasons for an act that seemed to me little short of madness. Forgetting that he had owed his safety to the very disguise and seclusion that were now both relinquished, he imagined that mixing with the inhabitants of Passages, like any other individual, would multiply the facilities of escape; and in this belief, had purchased a boat, in which himself and wife made daily, or rather nightly, excursions on the water, preparatory to that last, that was to convey them in safety, as he hoped, to the French coast.

It had not entered into Don Miguel's speculations that a Spanish boatman was an indispensable companion, and that the whole coast was scouted by Spanish vessels engaged in a scrutinizing blockade. In vain I pointed out the prudence of remaining quiet, at least until the movements of the Spanish forces were more accurately known, which might then allow of an escape by land to Bayonne, without approaching their hostile lines. In vain I pointed out the impossibility of escaping the scrutiny of a blockading force by sea. Obstinacy had planted his staff determined not to yield to reason; and thus I left them.

Preparations for an early renewal, on the following morning, of the embarkation of the Ordnance stores, kept me until a very late hour from my quarters. The night was moonless, and the irregular streets of Passages were so shrouded in darkness that I carried, as a necessary protection, a lanthorn to guide my steps.

The sound of voices in earnest conversation, and at so late an hour, made me, for a moment, hesitate whether to advance or retreat, and during that moment the guttural sounds of José's broken Spanish struck upon my ear.

Curiosity, and some strange feeling, undefinable, yet mysteriously powerful, caused me to retreat behind the jutting corner of an old building; but the colloquy, whatever it might have been, was closed. The parties walked away, their voices lowered to a whisper, and I had no alternative but to return, with curiosity unsatisfied, and suspicions strongly excited, to my own quarters. The door was opened to me by José, and though I turned the light of my lanthorn sharply on his face, in the hope of finding some traces that might solve my doubts, nothing was discernible beyond the half grin of quiet cunning that usually lurked there.

Early on the following morning, before leaving my quarters, I went to my Spanish friends to warn them of the danger that I believed threatened them, and to entreat them to resume their secluded life, until the dark clouds of their destiny had passed away. Donna Marguerita was occupied in concealing within a curiously wrought leathern belt some valuable jewels she had brought from Vittoria; while her husband, with fevered anxiety, told me that on the proceeding night, he had seen from a little window overlooking the narrow street, two men of very suspicious appearance in close conference with José; that a secret presentiment whispered that he was the subject of that conference, and that rather than live the prey to a thousand fears he had determined, on that night, to attempt an escape to the French coast. The boatman was engaged, the bark moored beneath the window, and to the blessed care of Virgin he would confide the rest.

During that day the embarkation of the Ordnance stores was completed, and my orders having been to repair to head-quarters at Lesaca, an opportunity was thus offered, not to be neglected, of getting José out of the way. I gave him directions to go off instantly to prepare my quarters at Lesaca; but I could not help fancying that there was at the time a sardonic laugh in his eye, that said as plainly as if he had spoken it, "I am a cleverer fellow than you are."

At sunset he started with one of my mules, and never did I feel much more relieved than when I saw his back fairly turned on my poor refugee guests. On that very day intelligence had been received of the arrest of two Spaniards of rank within the Spanish lines; both of whom had paid the penalty of their political backsliding with their lives, and this circumstance had increased my anxiety for the safety of my friends.

At about ten o'clock, I repaired to their apartment. The night was calm and beautiful, and as the rippling waves broke lazily and loud against the little boat beneath, it sounded, to my imagination, like a funeral dirge, moved by the prophetic spirit of the future. A figure wrapped in the dark cloak and flapping sombrero of the Spaniard, reclined indolently awaiting the party he was engaged to accompany. There was a pause of deep emotion, that wrung the hearts of that little party as they stood, gazing for the last time on the old wooden terrace, that looked too frail to bear even the weight of the delicate form, who was first to lead the way. One pressure of the hand, a stifled sob, a sigh, and the little boat, under its light sail, pressed onwards through the blue waters.

On my arrival at Lesaca, on the following morning, I found that José had played me false, and taken off, not only himself, but part of my baggage, and my best mule also. I could have borne my misfortunes more philosophically, had it not been for the anxious thought that would intrude of his absence being connected with the flight of my poor friends; and I caused him to be sought in all directions, but without avail. I never saw him afterwards!

The object of my going to Lesaca was to re-organize the several brigades of ammunition for the field, which the numerous actions that had taken place with the enemy—particularly those of the Pyrenees—had nearly exhausted.

From the 25th of July to the 2nd of August, the belligerent armies, with the exception of the blockading force at San Sebastian, under General Graham, had been in constant movement, during which period no less than ten actions had been fought; and perhaps there never was a similar test of the superiority of generalship than the mountainous locality of the Pyrenees afforded. On one side, the directing presence of the experienced Soult; on the other, the discerning, combining, and time-seizing spirit of Wellington. As force moved against force, retreating, advancing, dodging; as each Commander endeavoured by *finesse*, to outdo his skilful antagonist, the position of the armies represented in their different movements the scientific progress of a well-played game of chess, where each piece acts the parts assigned to it, under the powerful combination of man's intellectual agency. At the conclusion of these days of sanguinary hostilities the armies resumed their first position; the French occupied the hills about Ainhoa, the heights of Sarre, St. Jean de Luz, and St. Jean Pied de Port.

The line of the allied army extended from the pass of Roncesvalles to the mouth of the Bidassoa; the light division occupying the heights of Santa Barbara near to the little town of Vera.

CHAPTER VII

CAPTURE OF
SAN SEBASTIAN

ORDERS were now given for the renewal of the attack on San Sebastian, and for the relanding of the guns and stores, that for security had been embarked on board of transports in the harbour of Passages. The old guns, however, were found to have done their duty too efficiently to be in condition to begin again.

The unceasing vomiting of destructive missiles at the first attack on San Sebastian had not only caused the metal to droop at the muzzle, but had so enlarged the vents of the guns, that few of them were at all serviceable. We, therefore, waited for a fresh battering train from England, which arrived on the 20th of August, and also an abundant supply of small-arm ammunition. All was once more bustle and expectation; fatigue parties from the line, the artillery, and the navy, assisted in the disembarkation, and the scene presented one of stirring interest; nor was the picturesque wanting—the country boats we put in requisition, covering the blue waters of the little harbour, were manned, as Paddy might say, by Spanish women, whose dark expressive countenances, long plaited hair falling almost to the feet, and animated gestures, added a magical touch to the picture, that without it, would only have spoken to the heart of turbulence and strife.

During the suspension of the siege, the Governor of the Fortress had caused the defences and works to be repaired. New obstacles to the besiegers had been thrown up, and both men and ammunition were daily dropping in from Bayonne, owing to our naval force being inadequate to prevent it. On our side, the preparations for the premeditated attack were carried on far more vigorously than for the first. Sixty-three guns were planted on the right, and thirty-two on the left, making a total of ninety-five pieces of heavy ordnance, manned by the gunners from the field batteries, and amply supplied with ammunition. So matters stood till the 23rd, when the fire was opened on both sides, continuing with but little interruption until the 31st. Several times within that period, Lord Wellington visited the batteries in person, and for the last time on the 30th, when having carefully examined the state of the fortress, he gave orders that the assault should take place at eleven o'clock on the following morning.

Notwithstanding the dilapidated appearance of the outward defences, and inviting aperture of the gaping breach, the ingenious inventions of the besieged, to frustrate their assailants, were formidable; and as the sequel will show, accident alone effected what had baffled the almost super-human efforts of that terrible assault. Immediately behind the breach, a fall of twenty feet was the only means of entrance to the town beneath. This was defended by a high wall, grenelled for musketry, while the flanks of the summit of the breach, were defended by three lines of traverses, to prevent access to the connecting line of the ramparts. Mines were prepared to blow up the first adventurous spirits that might gain too firm a footing. Several pieces of Ordnance lay concealed, but ready to send forth their deadly missives on the assailants, and the heavy guns from the Mirador scowled upon the columns as they advanced from the trenches to the attack. From an eminence to the left of the howitzer battery, General Graham looked on, during which time I was with him, and therefore an eye-witness of the whole progress of the assault.

It was some time past eleven, when the Forlorn Hope, headed by the brave McGuire, rushed sharply to the breach. Close at its heels followed, like an impetuous torrent, the leading columns, under a fire of shot and shell that brought to the earth heaps of killed and wounded. As each succeeding party fell, so did another, and another, rush on with fearful shouts over the bodies of the slain, gaining the summit of the breach, and falling lifeless on it, as soon as gained; for the fearful leap below impeded further progress, and the impetuous assailants from the strand, could only cling to the crumbling walls, unable to advance, until the mighty current from behind forced them in turn upon the breach, in turn to die.

From the position in which General Graham stood, during this anxious and awful time, masses of our gallant fellows were to be seen ascending the broken fragments of the breach, and disappearing the moment afterwards to make room for succeeding victims, and yet no progress had been made. The breach and strand were strewn with heaps of slain, and up to that point, their gallant blood had flowed in vain. Occasionally the waving of an officer's sword, and the desperate efforts that followed, caused a momentary gleam of hope that was as suddenly checked by the increased fire of the besieged; and again the foot of the breach was covered with a fresh layer of unsuccessful dead.

To replace these losses, General Leith, who directed the assault, sent forth fresh columns of men, in rapid succession, but as these pushed with vigour from the trenches, the guns from the Mirador tore up their ranks, even before they gained the foot of the breach. Upwards of two hours and a half had elapsed since our gallant troops had been exposed to this terrible carnage, inflicted by an enemy, with whom they had no power of grappling in return.

At this crisis, it has generally been supposed that Sir Thomas Graham directed that our batteries should open fire upon the traverses, which flanked the great breach, and behind which were concealed the grenadiers, whose deadly musketry had contributed so much to the destruction of the besiegers. That such a measure was adopted is true, but it is equally so that the suggestion was made in my presence to General Graham by Colonel Dickson, whose experienced eye, and knowledge of the precision exercised by his gunners, made him foresee the advantages to be derived from it. Accordingly, the concentrated fire of fifty pieces of heavy Ordnance was turned upon the enemy's defences.

It would be difficult, indeed impossible, to describe the workings of the veteran Graham's stern countenance as he looked upon the sad destruction of his brave troops, but even this was for a moment forgotten in the interest that a new feature in the scene produced.

The sun shone with a brilliancy that gave to the burning sands in front of the batteries, the appearance of a spangled carpet, when suddenly there seemed to rise from it a close column of soldiers, arrayed in the dark uniform of the Portuguese.

Shooting rapidly to the right, they bore down towards the Arumea river, directly in front of the Mirador battery, while an officer, preceding by some yards the rest waving his sword and cheering on his men, plunged into the river that divided them from the small breach of the fortress.

As if paralysed at the bold attempt, the guns from the Mirador, and Monte Orguello ceased to fire; the smoke cleared off, and all eyes turned to the river, in which, above their waists in water, were wading, in close marching order, the devoted band.

A moment's pause ensued. Alas! it was but a moment, for the next brought a fierce flash from the Mirador, followed by a roar of fearful import, which showed too clearly that the momentary lull was but to insure the certainty of destruction by a more deadly aim. The white foam of the Arumea danced high into the air, while a dense cloud of black smoke rolled over the head of the column. Scarcely had it gained transparency, before a second discharge, more terrible than the first, fell in among them. An Oh! burst involuntarily from General Graham's lips, as he looked upon the murderous havoc made in the ranks of those brave men. Still, however, the survivors pushed on to the shore, and though assailed by a sharp fire of musketry from the ramparts, the gallant Major Snodgrass and his brave Portuguese followers succeeded in gaining the smaller breach of the fortress.

Yet still the death-winged missiles of the besieged continued with increasing intensity to carry destruction to the besiegers. All that human bravery could effect had been effected by our troops, and not an inch of real advantage gained. At this moment of feverish anxiety and uncertainty, a tremendous explosion, succeeded by several others, that seemed to shake the foundations of the earth, suddenly changed the aspect of affairs. A howitzer shell from our batteries had struck an expense magazine in the rear of the traverses, igniting an immense mass of combustible matter, live shells, &c. and blowing into the air numbers of the grenadiers who were placed behind the traverses to bar the entrance of the stormers from the town.

In every direction these hapless beings fell by the force of the explosion; legs and arms, heads, and headless bodies, showered over the ramparts among our men, who, shouting with exultation, rushed with frenzied enthusiasm to every crevice that offered admittance, proving how much the occurrence had contributed to renew the ardour of the attack. The ringing voice of the gallant Colonel Hunt, in leading on his heroes of the light division, was heard amidst the clamour of the fight, and the confusion of the enemy having paved the way to victory, the assailants rushed in like an impetuous torrent, at every point of entrance. The French contested the ground step by step, but in vain. The fortress was won; and as the British troops poured into the town, the only retreat left to the enemy was within the fortified position of Monte Orguello.

Thus, after a protracted siege, fell the Fortress of San Sebastian, leaving in its fall reflections of the most painful nature, whether we reflect on the noble men who shed their blood in the almost ferocious bravery that marked that assault, or whether we reflect on the whirl of evil passions that marked the foot-steps of the victors after the assault. Of the former, there were some, who will ever be remembered by those who knew them. One of the foremost of these was the brave McGuire. His beautiful countenance, as he lay stretched in the sleep of death at the foot of the breach, wore a sweet smile; and a calm serenity was spread over it, which seemed to say, "I have exchanged the bloody strife of man for the peacefulness of Heaven!"[1]

Who can ever forget McGuire who led the Forlorn Hope at San Sebastian?

The Engineers suffered severely. The commanding officer, Sir Richard Fletcher, who had gone through all the battlefields of the Peninsula, from the year 1808, with the regard and esteem of all men, fell, with several officers of his corps, before the breach of San Sebastian.

The pen shrinks from a description of the scene that succeeded to the capture of the fortress. On every side, in heaps, lay the dead and dying, while the frantic shouts of the incensed and excited soldiers, as they rushed into the town to glut their pent-up feelings of revenge upon everything that came in their way, mixed with the heavy rolling of a terrific thunder storm that swept down from the mountains. Nature seemed herself to mourn, not only over the extinction of some of her favourite spirits on that day, but over the influence that had been wrenched from her by the demon of revenge over the hearts of men.

For eight days succeeding the fall of the fortress, did the gallant Frenchman Rey, and his devoted garrison, hold out within their last remaining lines of defence; but sickness, famine, and the total destruction of their last bulwarks, necessitating their proud spirits to bend down: they surrendered prisoners of war,[2] and filed out with the honours of such, on the 9th of September, from a position that had taken us two months to subdue.

In a few short hours, the stillness of peace had replaced the din of war, but not so were the ravages of man to be obliterated; the town was in flames, the wretched inhabitants houseless and beggared, while many a defenceless woman with agonized heart, or maddened brain, bore witness to the still more horrible results of war.

1. Early on the morning of the assault, McGuire was seen dressed with unusual care, as if for some great occasion. Some one remarked upon it to him, when he replied, "When we are going to meet all our old friends whom we have not seen for many years, it is very natural to wish to look as well as possible."

2. The French officer, whose fearless exposure on the walls of the fortress, after the first attack, had been the means of preserving our wounded from the danger of our own guns, was restored unconditionally to liberty by Lord Wellington.

CHAPTER VIII

A TERRIBLE FATE

THE Ordnance stores were again to be embarked at Passages, and glad to escape from the spectacle of misery that every step presented, I found myself, towards evening, in my old quarters, overlooking the little harbour from the wooden terrace where I had last seen my Spanish friends.

The exciting scenes of San Sebastian had almost banished them from my mind, but when I entered the little room, where I had passed with them so many hours, I almost started to find it empty, and involuntarily my eyes turned to the wide expanse of ocean before me, as if I held it responsible for the safety of those, who had confided so much to its keeping. But how changed was the aspect of that ocean from the smiling face it wore on the night in question; scowling thunder clouds shed their dark reflection over what was then the deep blue water, and as the mighty waves came rolling in from the great Atlantic, chased by an equinoctial gale, each little bark and transport that rode at anchor in the harbour, shook and rocked to the wild music of the elements.

I stood on the old terrace, looking at the heightening storm, and watching, with intense interest, the many little sails that came dropping in to seek protection from the raging sea without. One by one they braved the buffeting of the waves, and landed their dripping owners on the beach, where many an anxious wife and mother stood to greet the welcome return. The wind had now risen to a fearful height, and far as the eye could reach, the fretted, agitated waters, rose like a huge bubbling cauldron, when distant

far was seen a *chasse-marée*, or country boat, making to the shore.
Every eye turned to the object with intense anxiety, not unmixed
with strong forebodings that neither seaman's skill, nor tight-set
boat could bear against that gathering storm.

The mariners collected on the shore, some to indulge in their
own speculations on the fate of the distant object, others with a
view to render assistance, if practicable. My elevated position from
the terrace, and English telescope, brought plainly to my view the
endangered bark. It was a fearful sight to witness the frail thing
at one moment tossed on the summit of a rising billow, the next
plunged into the abyss below, disappearing altogether between
the engulphing waves. So passed away some minutes, hope and
fear alternately prevailing, as the bark still rode on, diminishing,
at each plunge, her distance from the shore. A roll of mountain
waves now came hurling on her stern, and a shriek of terror burst
from the assembled women, as the avalanche swept over the tiny
atom—a deadly pause followed—and then a shout of gladness
as the boat popped up her head once more. As nearer and nearer
she approached the mouth of the harbour, so did dangers thicken
around her. The rolling waves that dashed with frantic fury against
the outward piles, rebounded back at the obstruction offered;
and, as if influenced by revenge, formed into whirling eddies,
threatening destruction to whatever might approach.

Again the wind, that had momentarily lulled, poured forth
the low and distant howl, that ushers in the ungovernable blast,
and in another moment the little sail flapped in ribbons over the
now unmanageable and death-doomed boat. With one bound
she reached the mouth of the harbour, but death was foremost in
the race, and at the same moment that by the growing darkness
three human figures were distinctly seen, with arms outstretched
to shore, the relentless waves struck on the side the gallant boat,
which sank to rise no more. A scream of horror rang from the
lookers-on that was re-echoed, as if in mockery, by the hissing
surge. But why does every heart beat again with hope as a small
dark spot becomes more discernible on the bosom of the waves?
One moment it is borne up on high, the next invisible; yet still
it re-appears, and nears the strand, while the thrilling voices with

which the men vociferate, "*Carracho*," and the women "*As Dios mio*," tell plainly that the frail strength of a human being is exerted against the strife of elements. Some brave fellows push off a boat in the direction of the object; a rope is thrown, and caught, and in a few seconds, a rescued man stands among his deliverers on the shore.

Turning from the dark storm without to the comforts of my canteen within, I sat me down to moralize upon the caprices of destiny. My mind pondered over the unequal measures meted out to man, and from which he traces the fiat, not only of his physical existence, but that of his moral also. In the wreck that I had witnessed, three human beings had suffered equally the terror of approaching death; two of them had been launched into that vast eternity, of which the element that betrayed them is, to mortal sight, the type. One had been saved—for what purpose? For what fate? Reserved to good or evil? To glorify on earth the divine hand that raised him from the "overwhelming waters?" Or to add another link to the chain that rivets Satan to the human race?

On the following morning, on leaving my quarters at an early hour, my attention was arrested by a crowd collected on the beach, and approaching to learn the cause, I found that the tide had thrown up the corpse of a woman, one of the victims, doubtless, of the previous night's storm, for accounts had already reached Passages of the total wreck of twelve vessels on the coast. Wrapped in a coarse cloak, the unconscious form lay in the arms of two boat men, the face entirely concealed by a mass of dark luxuriant hair, that fell, saturated by the heavy sea-water, like a funeral shroud over the inanimate clay, while from beneath the rough serge covering, peeped two exquisitely formed Andalusian feet, cased in materials too rich to belong to other class than that of gentle blood.

As I followed in the crowd to a neighbouring posado, where the body was to be deposited, I learnt that it had already been identified—by the man who had been saved on the previous evening—as that of a lady who perished with his fellow-boatman in entering the harbour of Passages. The hostess of the posado came out to receive the melancholy procession, and the still dripping body was placed upon a bed until the arrival of the Alcalde, who had been summoned to superintend the proceedings. The entrance of this dignitary was the signal for the removal of the cloak, and no sooner was this done, and the dark hair parted from the corpse, than the delicate and beautiful features of Donna Marguerita were exposed to view.

Round her waist, concealed by the black mantilla, that clung to her form in heavy folds, was the curious leathern belt, in which she had placed her valuables on the last day we met, and which the Alcalde now proceeded to open. A parcel of detached papers, bearing the direction of "Donna Flora," fell from the faithful deposit. One paper more the leathern belt contained, directed to myself. At the wish of the Alcalde, I opened it, and drew forth a woman's cambric handkerchief, steeped in blood. It told a tale that required not the confirmation of the few written words that were enclosed,—"*La sangue di marido asesinado!*"

All the information the boatman could give was, that a lady, apparently in great distress of mind, had engaged himself and another to take her in their boat to Passages. The rest we knew too well!

When the last mournful directions had been given respecting the interment of the body; and when the crowd had dispersed, to gather again together at the next passing object of idle curiosity, I gave to the Alcalde as much information regarding the hapless Don Miguel and his wife, as was consistent with my own position, and asked permission, which was easily granted, to be the medium of forwarding to Vittoria the papers addressed to Donna Flora by her unfortunate relative. They were unsealed, and open; and as I knew they could only relate to those circumstances with which I was acquainted, I did not hesitate, on my return to my quarters, to peruse them.

Once again, and for the last time, I found myself in the room they had occupied; the door leading to the terrace was open, and behind it, like a framed picture, lay the sea, as calm and as blue as on that night when the little boat waited beneath the window; while the rippling waves that now struck against the landing place, reminded me of the requiem they then seemed to chaunt over those beings that futurity was committing to their agency.

Tears had turned to blots the unconnected and scarcely discernible words that lay before me, traced by the trembling hand of Donna Marguerita, and yet the purport was too plain. The revengeful José had been the traitor; leagued with the boatman, the latter had run the little bark on the hostile beach of Andaye, where the Judas was himself in waiting—and not alone.

Under an escort of Spanish *partidas*, the unhappy fugitives were conducted to a near post of the Spanish army, where the Conde was tried for treason on the spot, and summarily shot in the presence of his agonized wife.

I was present at the interment of Donna Marguerita, and caused the handkerchief, that her enthusiastic affection for her husband had dipped in his blood, to be laid beside her in the silent tomb. "*Requiescat in pace.*"

CHAPTER IX

WAR AMONG THE MOUNTAINS

DURING the assault of San Sebastian, Marshal Soult attacked the position of the allied army at Vera, in the hope of being able to bring relief to the distressed Governor of San Sebastian. It is difficult to assign any reason for Soult having deferred this attempt until the moment when it may be said that the assailants were in the breach, unless that his information respecting the progress of the siege was at variance with the fact.

Before reaching Oyerzum, from whence a good road led to the beleaguered fortress, the French Marshal had to force the passage of the Bidassoa, to pass the lofty mountains of San Marcial, the Pena de Haya, and the heights of Vera, opposed at every step by an army, superior in strength to his own. The consequence was a long and sanguinary struggle, its terrors heightened by a tremendous hurricane, not unfrequent in the wild and elevated regions of the Pyrenees.

The combat waged fierce and bloody on these mountain tops. In the distance, for many miles, the hills and rocks looked alive with the moving groups that crowned them. As far as the eye could reach, the dark smoke curled densely on their sides and summits, while the pealing musketry reverberated in sullen repetition through the echoing crags. Here and there the dark red fire might be seen flashing from the cannon's mouth, its deep roar mingling with the shouts of the allied troops, as they drove the French down the mountain slopes they had too rashly ascended, forcing them to recross the boundary stream of the Bidassoa, swollen into a dangerous torrent, by the rush of descending waters, impelled by the hurricane above.

The loss on both sides was severe, that of the allied army being estimated at nearly three thousand; and of the French at four thousand men. But far more than the loss of four thousand men was sustained by the enemy in this desperate onset. The morale of the French army had been already weakened by a succession of defeats; and here was another, affording, as it seemed, an unnecessary display of declining strength. Driven to the very threshold of their own country, the soldiers felt the humiliation of their position; no longer imbued with the daring spirit that animates an invading army, they beheld themselves on the point of becoming, by stringent necessity, the defenders of their own soil from invasion.

A foreign foe was already on the frontier mountains, looking down with the laugh of triumphant derision on the broad plains of France; hence the wild impetuous rush to protract, at least, the dreaded encroachment. A movement that probably originated more from the vehement desire of action, than from any reasonable hope of averting definitively the impending evil.

On those mountain heights stood the Spaniards, no longer flying in terror before the French troops, or skulking to their mountain fastnesses like outlaws in their native land. No longer defenceless victims to the brute force of a savage multitude that despised their weakness, and held cheap their courage; that time had passed away, and a goodly array of well-armed men, in all the strength of discipline, stood prepared to glut a retributive vengeance in their turn.

The Portuguese likewise—they, for whom the French had evinced so utter a contempt—they also stood on those mountain tops, a brave and daring band, not only looking down upon the distant plains of France with hopes of a nearer acquaintance with them, but prepared to tread their way through paths of blood, if necessary, to reach them. In proof of this, so desperate was their bayonet charge at the bridge of Lesaca, that the French, humiliated at their repulse by men they had so despised, vehemently asserted that British soldiers had fought in the uniform of the Portuguese.

What a glorious tribute from an enemy to British valour! at the same time showing how the good effects of British discipline had gradually extended to troops, that at one time were more dangerous than useful as auxiliaries in the field. Here then was a powerful army, strong both in numbers and efficiency, eagerly waiting for the coming crisis.

The sanguinary strife of the preceding months had produced a daily association with death, that had weakened its terrors in the minds of those engaged in it. Each felt that his turn was perhaps the next, and a kind of apathetic indifference was the result. There was also another cause to reconcile survivors to the loss of friends, in despite of the excellent fellowship that existed between all ranks of men in the Peninsula, and pre-eminently among the "choice spirits" of the light division. The death of an officer gave a step of promotion in the regiment, and therefore the senior Captain, who stepped into a majority, or the senior Lieutenant who obtained his company, found in that circumstance a healing balm to his regret.

It was of usual occurrence to hear the young officers, when assembled after an engagement, congratulating themselves on the promotion that had perhaps fallen in among them, with the explosion of some murderous shell.

In the 95th regiment, there were two brothers, the eldest was a Captain; the youngest a Lieutenant in the same battalion, and such was the avidity of the former for promotion, that although an excellent fellow, he would have seen all the officers in his regiment spitted like larks, if such a process would have given "a step," as he used to term it, either to himself or to his brother "Joe." At every fresh casualty that occurred—and there were many, for the gallant 95th was always in action—the Captain would exultingly exclaim, if the deceased was a superior officer to himself "poor fellow! he was a good fellow, *but*, it is a step for me." If junior to himself; his fraternal affection found an equal pleasure in saying, "poor fellow! he was a good fellow, *but*, it is a step for Joe," and so frequently were these expressions used, that they became play-words in the regiment.

During the heat of the combat at the bridge of Vera, a ball struck the Captain to the earth, but as he related the story himself, not very long after, it is unnecessary to add, that promotion had not yet done with him.

For a long time he lay unconscious of the war that waged around, nor recovered his senses until all was over, and a sergeant and some men had approached to remove the bodies of their comrades from the ground. Although faint and unable to stir from the effects of his wounds, he was still able to remember that the sergeant advanced to the spot where he lay, and pointing with commiseration to his apparently dead body said: "Ah Jack, there lies our poor Captain!" The soldier apostrophised, quickly retorted with a laugh: "Poor fellow! he was a good fellow; but it is a step for Joe!"

It did not fall to the good fortune of all, on that day, to be removed from the field of suffering in the manner of this gallant lover of promotion. Many lingered, in hopeless agony, until death came like a friend to their relief; others were brought into hospital, on the third day, and yet recovered, although the pangs of starvation, and exposure to the weather had terribly aggravated the condition of their wounds. Some poor fellows were never found, nor afterwards heard of, having no doubt fallen victims to the plundering fiends that infest all battlefields.

An instance occurred of a brave officer of the 34th regiment who was seen to fall wounded among the mountain brushwood; the spot was marked by the lifeless bodies of some soldiers of his regiment. At the cessation of the combat, a party was sent to find the wounded man, headed by the individual who had seen him fall. The place was identified by many tokens, but he they sought was no longer there.

In vain they explored the neighbouring hills, and tore away the dwarf trees, to which he might have crawled for shelter. The search was unavailing, although it proved that he had been there, for a torn pocket handkerchief, bearing his initials, was found hanging to a bramble bush, close to the spot where he was last seen.

For a long time afterwards, it was hoped that the poor fellow had fallen into the hands of the French, and would be spared to recount the history of his escape; but time at length crushed such hopes, and it was then conjectured that some wolfish being had stripped the sufferer, and hurled him down the precipice into the torrent beneath.

At the bridge of Vera, a party of the 95th gallantly defended the pass, and Captain Cardew, a veteran officer of the regiment, nobly fell in this encounter with the enemy. He was much beloved; and as conspicuous for valour in the field, as for his gentle courtesy out of it. I had received orders to repair to Lesaca, the head-quarters of the army, on a particular duty, and arrived just as the sale of poor Cardew's goods and chattels was in progress. Truly it is a melancholy sight to witness the regimental process of the disposal of articles, that look as if they formed part and parcel of the owner himself.

As I entered, the half worn-out jacket, and still glittering chacot were held up to view by the military auctioneer. Such objects usually go in the regiment, and bidders were not slack in their endeavours to obtain some relic of their lamented comrade. In some short moments, the limited wardrobe was dispersed in divers hands, and with the exception of the sword and watch, reserved as mementos for sorrowing relatives, all other things fell piece-meal into the hands of those, who were in daily intercourse and friendly association with the deceased.

Only a few hours before, and the gallant Cardew stood, on that very spot, reconnoitering with his glass the mountain heights at the foot of which he now lay a mangled corpse. But such is the fate of war. His death was the birth of grief to some fond hearts; but to his regiment "A step for Joe."

CHAPTER X

THE BIDASSOA

ON the morning of the 7th of October, the allied army moved against the French, and after a day's hard fighting, effected the passage of the Bidassoa, causing the enemy to retreat back to his position. Nothing could surpass the conduct of our troops on that occasion; and though the complicated and difficult details of warfare, carried on amidst the gigantic mountains of the Pyrenees have been already described by historians as accurately as the locality will permit, there were patches of home scenery, so to speak, that could only fall beneath the individual eye.

The dark green jackets of Barnard's rifles, as they fought their way in climbing up the steep and rugged hills, whose summits were crowned by the enemy; the bright red and white colours of the 43rd and 52nd, as they crossed, in close column, the valley which divided the heights they had quitted from those they sought to gain; and then, throwing off their kits, in single file, wound up the narrow broken paths that led them to the fierce expecting foe, whose peppering fire from above seemed only to infuse fresh vigour into those unrivalled "Light Bobs;" the aspect of the Spaniards, whose sombre hues made it difficult to distinguish them from the brown rocks, over which they clambered with the characteristic agility of the inhabitants of mountainous countries,—all these were brilliant lights and shades in the great picture of nature's wilderness before us.

The 52nd, led by Major William Mein, on reaching the brow of the mountain, formed rapidly into line, and without firing a single shot, advanced in double quick time against a column of the

enemy, which had only a few minutes before driven a regiment of
Portuguese Cacadores over the other side of the rugged declivity.
The soul-inspiring cheer that rang from the ever foremost 52nd,
struck terror into the ranks of the French, they wavered, as British
steel advanced. Then turned and fled towards one of their great
redoubts; they were so closely pursued, that some of the 52nd
actually entered the redoubt, with their flying foes, upon which
the latter again started forth from the opposite side, making,
at the top of their speed towards a second line of redoubts and
entrenchments.

On the right of the first redoubt, was a deep and thickly wooded
ravine, in which a body of three or four hundred of the enemy
was concealed; but being discovered, some companies of our rifles
advanced at a running pace, by a little footpath, parallel to the
ravine, to intercept their sortie. The French within the ravine also
ran to reach the opening first, and a regular race took place between
them. The view holloa of the rifles, as they spied their enemies
through the trees, rang through the air, and with renewed spirit they
bounded over the narrow footway, reaching the mouth of the ravine
at the same moment as the French. The latter, panic-struck at so
close a proximity with the green jackets, threw down their arms and
surrendered as prisoners of war. Their commanding officer was a fine
lively young fellow, and it was difficult to prevent him from jeering
and laughing at the volley of "carrachos" that the Spaniards fired
at him when within their power. Moreover, they were so disposed
to handle him roughly, that we recommended him in kindness,
to bridle his tongue, as no influence would have been available in
protecting him from the carbines of the Spaniards. With ourselves,
he was both courteous and gentle in return for some kindness that
was shown to him. His arm had been broken by a musket ball, and I
remember that one of our young officers converted his own pocket-
handkerchief into a sling, while others tore up theirs for bandages,
until surgical assistance could be had.

The result of this day's fighting, though the loss on both sides
was severe, was the opening of the passage of the Bidassoa to the
allied armies, and thus, a firmer footing was gained upon the
frontiers of France.

CHAPTER XI

MY BILLET AT VERA

AFTER the victory gained in the passage of the Bidassoa, the head-quarters of the army removed to Vera, a small village still more embedded than Lesaca in the mountain wilderness. My billet was in the house of the parish priest, and in these days of religious contumacy, when, in our favoured land, it is a matter of frequent occurrence to witness the feuds and dissensions that embroil the church, when shepherds and their flocks seem united but on the one point of seeking causes for disunion, in such days as these, memory furnishes a refreshing contrast in Padre Oliveira, the parish priest of Vera. Upon a stipend that would sound strange to the ears of our well-paid Rectors, this holy man was rich among his parishioners, but above all, he was rich in the charity that he dispensed spiritually and temporally to his attached flock.

The modest parsonage was close to the little church, whose tiny steeple, as it reared its head among the stupendous rocks and elevated mountains, was no unfitting representation of pigmy man, in communion with the mysteries of eternity. The Padre's home was under the guidance of a sister, many years younger than himself; an arrangement that removed from the little dwelling the comfortless aspect that domiciles exhibit, in nine cases out of ten, when deprived of female vigilance and care. Next to his parishioners, the simple-hearted man loved best his bees; from bees to flowers, the step is short, but with him it led to still higher researches, and as a botanist and naturalist, Padre Oliveira was held in no mean repute.

The little apartment allotted to me was scrupulously neat. It had been furnished by himself, and although plain, evinced a degree of taste, shewing how much alike, though perhaps differing in nation, language, and religion, are those in whom purity of mind dwells as an habitual principle, diffusing its mild effulgency over every minutiæ of life. Such purity as this dwelt in the good Padre, and he and his mountain home were well suited to each other, protected by the little church that looked like a link in that dreary nature between himself and a more beautiful world.

The room that I occupied led by a narrow passage to a door that opened on a little flower-garden; beyond it was the church. The autumn was already considerably advanced, and in those mountain regions the rushing wind howled in mournful cadence, shaking the dry leaves into noises that sounded unearthly in the stillness of the night.

I had several times fancied that I heard the sound of footsteps in the passage leading to my room, but the gusts of wind would return with terrific violence and drive such thoughts away. At length, from long continuance, these hurricanes ceased to disturb me, and I slept soundly to their boisterous lullaby.

The placid equanimity of my worthy host seemed proof against all storms, either from within or from without, and his sister, the quiet Agnese, was like the waters of a lake on a summer evening, that deep and motionless receive the reflection of external objects on their bosom, but are incapable of disclosing of their own. No characters are so difficult to fathom as the apparently apathetic. The more complete the stagnation of the moral existence, so long as the ordinary events of every-day life have been alone concerned, the more terrific has been known the sudden rousing of the soul to violent action by some untouched spring; but to return to the good curate and his quiet sister. Few had been the words exchanged between this young woman and myself beyond what the courtesies of civilized life required, and in truth there was something in her manner discouraging to a nearer acquaintance.

Unlike the generality of her countrywomen, Agnese was delicately fair, with a profusion of flaxen ringlets, her light coloured eyes were only remarkable for their passionless lustre, and as she flitted from room to room, in pursuance of her domestic duties, invariably attired in a flowing dress of white fustian, she appeared the very personification of the "Lady of Avenel," or the better known, because more modern, "Dame Blanche". There was also a strange expression in those pale eyes, as they wandered from object to object, without seeming to know where to rest; shunning the look that would have detained them for a moment on their unquiet progress.

Between the reverend father and his young relative, there was as little of congeniality as between herself and me. The daily duties of his profession took him much from home, but on his return, no step of joyful recognition bounded to his fraternal embrace, the presence of youth was unfelt, with all its gladdening attributes, that usually break down the barriers that age and sober reason would raise against them; the quiet Agnese was there, but cold, passive, indifferent as an automaton under the control of machinery.

At the hospitable, but frugal, evening meal, I was sometimes a guest, and should have been so more frequently, but for the strange feelings that the presence of Agnese invariably produced in me; her whole appearance was so strange and unearthly, she ate so sparingly, that imperceptibly, I had identified her in my imagination with the female Ghoul in the Arabian Nights, picking rice by single grains in the day-time, and satisfying her cravings with less delicate fare at night. At an early hour, the Padre usually concluded his day of usefulness by a short prayer, the benediction of Heaven was invoked on the inmates of his dwelling, and we severally retired to be rocked into repose by the bellowing winds from the adjacent mountains.

November, dreary November had set in, and Vera was still the head-quarters of Lord Wellington, but since the successful issue of the 7th of November, the army had been thrown into a position still nearer to the French territory; and although nothing was positively made known as to its intended movements, there was sufficient to guarantee the certainty of an aggressive advance upon the enemy being in contemplation. In support of this assurance, the first days of November were employed by Lord Wellington in moving the several corps of the army into position, preparatory to his attack on Soult, and every breast beat high with expectancy that the approaching crisis would lead to the immediate invasion of southern France. We had received orders to march on the 9th from Vera, and mine excellent host had indulged his kind nature by preparing sundry articles of dainty fare for the occasion. The weather had become mild and rainy, and the monotonous trickling of the water from the roof, had replaced the noisy howling of the wind. Again I fancied that each night brought the return of those sounds I had attributed to the creaking beams of the old house shaken by the blast. One night I felt assured that footsteps were approaching. I listened attentively, they seemed to recede, a door opened, gently closed, and all was still. The following night, at the same hour, I heard the same sounds; again I listened, they became more distant, a door opened and closed. Curiosity was too powerful to remain unsatisfied. I, therefore, opened my own door, and stole—I am half ashamed to own it—on tip-toe to the end of the passage. Another moment assured me beyond a doubt that two persons, of different sexes, were together within a few yards of where I stood. The voice of Agnese was of too remarkable a quality to be mistaken for another's. It was a thin and wiry voice, such as might have been expected from so chilling a reservoir—but who was he, the visitor to a young girl's virgin chamber at that unholy hour? I heard him whisper. Could it be in accents of love to such an icicle as Agnese! Again I listened. She spoke with all the warmth of awakened passion—yet still her voice grated harshly on my ear, as some voices do, leaving a chiming knell that vibrates painfully on the nerves.

Unwilling to play a protracted part of eaves-dropper, I retreated to my own apartment. Not a sound disturbed the stillness of the night, beyond the dull pattering of the rain upon my windows, and the sullen blackness of the sky was uncheered by a single star. Long and patiently I watched for further tokens of the nocturnal visitor's presence, but sleep will beset the faculties of the most curious; and so in my case. After tiring myself out with speculations and surmises, all of them, it must be admitted, most unchivalrously prejudicial to the fair Agnese's fame, I fell asleep, and so ended my disquisitions on the subject.

During the whole of the next day, I was occupied in extensive arrangements for completing the several mule brigades of small arm ammunition that were to move with the troops, and therefore had little time to ponder on the events of the preceding night, or even to see my host and his sister, until the hour of supper. It was with no kindly scrutiny that I bent my eyes on Agnese, as she coldly and silently performed the honours of the table during this evening meal. My feelings towards her were changed to positive dislike, from the innate conviction—a kind of presentiment that is always conclusive to the heart, because it springs from the heart—that she was betraying the confidence of her unsuspecting brother.

The conversation turned chiefly upon my approaching departure; the state of Spain; the increasing resources of the allied army, and tottering position of Soult, driven back to the verge of his own frontier boundary. From politics we travelled onwards to the condition of the Church of Rome in Spain; her decadency in concentrated force since the first invasion of the French, which, however, had only tended to the increase of her power; for, in those days of trouble, each parish priest invested himself in his restricted circle, with the authority and infallibility that in ordinary times, were arrogated by the Pope exclusively; and thus the discipline of the church was maintained in all its rigidity.

Notwithstanding the benign nature of my host, it was not difficult to see that he looked upon me as a heretic, though destined perhaps at the eleventh hour to be received into the bosom of the Holy Church; and he much lamented that I had not had the benefit of frequent conferences with the holy brother Antonio, a member of the Franciscan Monastery on the road to Araquil, whose erudition and piety were celebrated throughout the whole of northern Spain. As the worthy man pursued his eulogium of brother Antonio with all the warmth of religious zeal and admiration, my eyes accidentally turned on the countenance of Agnese. Was it indeed her, or another? I gazed and gazed again; the paleness of her cheeks had given place to a tint of vermilion; the usually insipid eyes were lit up with a fire that seemed to expend itself in rays of dazzling light;

she was beautiful to look upon; but there was something awful in her beauty.

After our little party broke up, I found myself in my sleeping chamber, entangled in a maze of wild thoughts; the fatigues of the day were, however, an effectual counterpoize even to my curiosity, and I fell asleep, in spite of all my resolutions to solve the mystery that perplexed me. Perhaps I should never have been the wiser on the subject, if chance, that ready waiting-maid to fortune, had not helped me ever beyond my expectations or desires.

The grey dawn of a November morning was just tinting the gloomy sky, when the closing of a door roused me from my sleep. I started up; and this time went to the window, that overlooked the Padre's garden. A tall figure habited in the frock and cowl of a friar, was rapidly moving in the direction of the church that formed a boundary to this small plot of ground. With a key he turned the lock of the entrance door and disappeared within its walls. Here then was another step gained towards the development of this strange mystery. Yet could it be possible, I asked myself, that a young girl, brought up in the simplicity of a rural life, and the rigidity also, of the Roman Catholic faith; should receive a nightly visitor, and that visitor in the garb of a monastic fraternity? Both reason and feeling argue strongly against the probability of such a circumstance, and I felt relieved by my reflections, and determined, for the future, to set down all mysterious movements that I might see, to the account of some mystical religious observances, that my heresy prohibited me from being initiated in.

On the afternoon of the same day, I returned from the completion of my duties to partake of an early farewell dinner with my host. Orders had arrived for the breaking up of head-quarters on the following morning. The whole army was in motion, and a great battle was evidently on the eve of taking place. With such a prospect in view, it may be supposed that little room was left in the mind for subjects unconnected with it, and it required nothing less than the extraordinary events that occurred during the last few hours of my stay at Vera to have rivetted them in my memory with a strength that time has not weakened.

On entering the little parlour that served both as dining-room and study to the Padre, I found he was not alone, and it required but a single glance at the tall figure that meekly rose, and saluted me, to recognize the friar that I had seen under such ambiguous circumstances. My simple host smiled triumphantly at the surprise I was unable to conceal, and which he attributed, poor man! to my reverence for the name by which he introduced his guest,— the reverend brother Antonio.

Had the eulogium I had already heard passed upon this individual been confined to the external man, it would have fallen far short of the truth, for rarely, if ever, had it been my lot to witness so perfect a delineation of human beauty. The shorn hair, that marked his holy calling, might almost have been deemed a *ruse* of art, to display the intellectual contour of the head; while the lofty forehead, polished as Carrara marble, and fringed with the thickset sable locks, spoke to the imagination of abstract science, midnight vigils, and the student's toil. Nor were the features of the countenance less perfect than the head; the eyes dark, luminous, and searching. The nose of the truest Grecian mould; the mouth and chin full, and what a Lavater might have named voluptuous; yet the vacant, brutish expression of the voluptuary was not to be traced in that brilliant and beautiful face.

I learnt from my host that the sudden illness of his sister was the cause of the friar's visit to the house. Agnese had expressed a wish to see the holy Antonio, to whom the guidance of her religious principles had been entrusted by her brother, and the latter was the more anxious to accede to her wish, from Antonio being versed in the science of medicine, and in the qualities of healing herbs, that were never known to fail, when administered by himself.

To lessen the anxiety of the brother, the friar consented to remain until the evening, which came too soon to put an end to the charms of his conversation. The variety of his knowledge was as surprising as the depth of thought, which he seemed to have bestowed upon every subject. His beautiful quotations from classical authors were relieved by an equally perfect conversancy with modern languages and their literature; his manners were a mixture of the frankness that springs from nature, and the polished reserve which characterizes the man of good society.

On the subject of politics, he evinced the independent spirit that spurns at tyranny, and claims for the human race the heaven-born gift of freedom. On that of religion, his liberal mind admitted no pale of division between man and his Creator; and the flush that for a moment lighted up the cheek of our pious host, as if in gentle reproach at the unexpected boldness of such an avowal, was answered by a warm effusion of blood over the beautiful countenance, which seemed almost to speak the words: "All men are brothers."

So completely had this singular person carried away my best feelings in his favour, that when he rose to take his leave, and after cordially embracing his friend, extended his hand to myself, I confess that all thoughts of Agnese, and deception, were wafted from my mind like chaff before the wind.

CHAPTER XII

THE MIDNIGHT BURIAL

THE night that precedes the commencement of a march is always one of bustle and excitement; and, on this occasion, my time was occupied until the last moment in looking over the returns of ammunition in the field for the ensuing conflict. This pressure of official business prevented me from taking repose that night, and led to a discovery that initiated me into one great feature of worldly knowledge—a distrust in appearances.

Twelve o'clock, that hour for all dismal stories and hob-goblin terrors, was striking by the church clock, and my pen was seeking the ink-stand in a lazy, and half-tired manner, when my ear caught the sound of footsteps in the passage, followed by the closing of a door. I jumped up, determined this last night to make the most of my time, and following the sound, found myself once more playing the part of Paul Pry at the door of a young lady's apartment.

Again I heard, at intervals, the voice of Agnese, but in faint and feeble tones, while suppressed moans, the evident tokens of severe suffering, showed that the malady of the patient had gained ground since the previous evening. The deep voice of the friar announced that she was not without the aid her situation required; and I, therefore, returned to my own room, and tried to resume my writing, but an unaccountable agitation rendered this no easy task, and propelled by an irresistable impetus, I retraced my steps to the passage. At the instant that I reached the door of Agnese's apartment, a faint cry, not to be mistaken, the first that weakness utters on the threshold of this world of sin and sorrow, rang clearly and even sharply through the air. It was the first and last evidence of life!

Another hour elapsed, and the door leading to the garden opened gently on its hinges. I hastily extinguished the light that might have betrayed me, and stationed myself at the window. The night was so intensely dark, that it was impossible to discern the nearest object; but while vainly straining my eyes to catch the tall figure of the friar, a dull light suddenly fell upon a patch of earth beneath the church wall at the extremity of the garden. It was evidently produced by a dark lanthorn, and by a strange misconception of its effects, the deed that darkness was intended to conceal, was rendered visible. The tall figure of the friar was no longer shrouded in the gloom of night, and without being able to account for it, my blood ran cold as I looked upon him.

The earth was saturated with the heavy rains, and it required but little exertion to make an aperture in her moistened bosom. A shovel in the friar's hands performed this work most expeditiously, but guilt is seldom accompanied by self-possession, and even this accomplished hypocrite tarried in his work, to look around in fear. At length, the task was done, and a little grave stood yawning for its intended occupant. Nor did it wait long. Another hurried look around him, and then, drawn from beneath the cowled frock, an infant—murdered, there is little doubt, by the author of its being—was transferred to that silent bed.

The friar, after replacing the earth, and trampling it to a level surface, stood for a moment motionless. How were his thoughts engaged in that brief space?

CHAPTER XIII

BATTLE OF THE NIVELLE

BEFORE sunrise on the morning that opened with the event recorded in the last chapter, I left Vera, and before the close of the same day, the battle of the Nivelle had added its lustre to the British arms.

On that morning the two belligerent armies again stood in hostile array amidst the stupendous mountains of the Pyrenees. The rich valleys of France lay stretched below to stimulate both sides; the one to a victory that would lead to those smiling plains; the other to a victory that would save them from an invading and triumphant foe.

The combatants stretched along a chain of mountains, extending over nearly fifteen miles, and were more numerous on both sides than in any former action of the Peninsula; the French counting eighty thousand, the Anglo-Portuguese and Spaniards ninety thousand men.

Our artillery, under Colonel Dickson, consisted of ninety-five guns, in a perfect state of efficiency, besides a mountain battery of three-pounders, directed by Lieutenant Robe. The latter were not, perhaps, capable of doing much mischief, but the moral effect they produced of alarm as their shot came tumbling down from the cloud-topped hills, was fraught with consequences still more important.

The able historian, who has handed down to posterity the workings of that mountain strife, has fertilized the crags and rugged cliffs of the Pyrenees with the brave blood that bathed them. What more could be added to the already recorded tales of daring deeds that passed in those grand recesses of nature's solitude, where even her sternest barriers were spurned and conquered by the resolute and enthusiastic ardour of our British troops.

Where all are nobly brave, it seems almost a wrong to specify a part, but just as among the beauteous stars of Heaven, we look most at those that shed the brightest light, so may we without detracting from the rest, single out from among the heroes of the Nivelle, Colborn's light brigade. Gigantic rocks were fitting tombstones for such men.

The victory of our troops was complete; the forces of Soult were driven from their position, and on the same night, San Pé became the head-quarters of Lord Wellington, and his first stepping stone on the soil of France.

CHAPTER XIV

WOUNDED FRENCHMEN

ON the morning that succeeded the battle, I rose early from my bivouac on the mountain of Sarre, and prepared to start, in pursuance of orders, for the ground lately occupied by the enemy. My duty was to ascertain the extent of the artillery captured, and the means to be employed for collecting it; and mounting my horse, I advanced in the direction of a range of high mountains, which appeared in the distance accessible only to the chamois and mountain goat.

The difficulty I found in ascending to the summit of the first ridge of hills was well repaid by the beauty of the view, which opened over an extensive line of country. Mountains and vallies lay in wild confusion, while the deep ravines, clothed with amber-coloured carpets of wild broom, relieved the sober tints of pine and fir with which that country abounds. The recent rains had swollen the mountain streams into torrents, and in many places, where their course was impeded by the jutting rocks, that boldly rose in perpendicular heights, the waters, as if indignant at the obstacles presented to their progress, rushed furiously in their fall from crag to crag, in every beautiful variety of shape and hue.

On reaching the valley, pure and placid streams branched out from their raging bosom, and winding through the fertile plains, appeared, from the heights whence I viewed them, like silver threads in the sun's rays. The sides of many of the mountains were thickly wooded with all the varieties of foliage that distinguish Pyrenean scenery, and although approaching winter had thrown over nature a veil of gloom; yet here and there autumnal beauty lingered.

The ascent and descent of each mountain now became more and more arduous and intricate, as if nature, in this vast retreat, had intended to exclude her enemy, man; and it was after several hours, in which I had made comparatively but little progress over the short firs and stunted shrubs which covered the ground, that I found myself on the summit of a high mountain, overlooking a valley, which arrested my attention.

The waters of the Nivelle intersected a broad and fertile plain, and on every side lofty mountains reared their towering heads, one above another, forming a natural boundary that seemed to preclude all possibility of egress from the valley. It was a spot that Johnson might have selected for his Rasselas. Dotted here and there upon the surrounding heights were huts, curiously and carefully constructed of turf, and of trees closely interwoven together. I quickly recognized them as the work of men who were adepts in campaigning life, and taking a rugged path that led in the direction of these temporary abodes, I found myself in the midst of an encampment of the enemy. The scene was one of interest; here and there lay stretched, in the appalling stillness of death, the victims of the preceding day's strife, and in the distance might be heard the noisy merriment of those who were perhaps destined, before many days were over, to meet with a similar fate.

I soon found myself surrounded by French soldiers, who, at the first onset were disposed to survey me with no very kindly feeling; but as soon as it was established satisfactorily to them that I was alone, and perhaps separated like themselves by the chances of war from the main body of the army, a cordial welcome was proffered me. The hard features of the grenadiers relaxed from their severity, and an officer politely offered me to partake of his flask of brandy, which was all he had to offer. The poor fellows were sadly in want of provisions as well as surgical assistance, and I promised, if it lay in my power, to send them relief.

The wounded lay in groups of three and four on the ground; some of them had their heads bandaged up with handkerchiefs, that showed by their crimson dye, the severity of the wounds they covered. Others had torn strips from their clothes to support a mutilated limb; others, again were too far gone to alleviate their miseries by such means, and were seeking insensibility to suffering, through the dram-bottle of that most unfeminine of the feminine gender yclep'd *vivandière*, whose spiritual aid was all the sufferers had to solace them here below.

Having reiterated my promise to send whatever assistance fell in my way, I was preparing to examine the redoubts, where the guns were in position, when a weak voice, in suffering accents of entreaty, pronounced a few words in English, that made me turn to the spot from they came. Against a bank I saw reclining, a wounded veteran officer, in the uniform of a Chasseur regiment. Care, rather than time, seemed to have ploughed deep furrows on his high and thoughtful forehead.

A few white hairs, thinly scattered over a head, that for its form might have been coveted by the speculative Spurzheim, contrasted strangely with his black eyebrows, and dark, unshaven beard. The shadows of death were gradually overspreading his countenance. As I approached nearer to the place where he lay, another object became visible, which the bank had before concealed; on the other side of the wounded man, lay a large black poodle dog, of that peculiarly clever breed that puts to the blush the boasted supremacy of man's intellectual faculties over the brute creation. Upon his master's drooping eye, the animal gazed with an expression of deep devotion and despair.

As I leant over the bank, which supported the sinking frame of the old soldier, he tried to raise himself, and placing his hand upon his breast, as if by the movement to delay the inward progress of dissolution, he said to me, "If you are an English officer, you can give me comfort in my dying hour. Yesterday I had a son, we were in the same regiment, and fought side by side; twice he saved my life by turning aside the bayonet that threatened it, and when at last I fell, he tried to bear me to a place of safety, but at the moment, the enemy bore down upon our ranks, and I was separated in the *mêlée* from my gallant boy. Should he be a prisoner in your army, for the sake of humanity, endeavour to discover his destination, and convey to him these papers."

With a feeble effort, the dying soldier placed in my hands a packet addressed to "Maurice McCarthy, sous-lieutenant au 8ème regiment de Chasseurs." The clouds of approaching dissolution were rapidly gathering over his face, as he still endeavoured, at broken intervals, to give some clue to guide me in my search.

He was an Irishman, had entered the French army after the rebellion in Ireland, and had served with Napoleon both in Italy and Egypt. I staid with him as long as it was possible, but the call of duty was peremptory, and I was obliged to quit the poor fellow to pursue the object of my journey.

He grasped my hand when we parted, and as I turned to take a last look at him in the distance, I could see the close contact, into which the faithful dog had brought himself with his master's body, as if to mingle warmth with the frigidity of life's last struggles.

CHAPTER XV

A SLIGHT MISUNDERSTANDING

MY object in exploring the ground that had been occupied by the enemy was to ascertain the quantity of artillery that had been abandoned, which consisted of fifty-two guns, and a considerable quantity of ammunition. The extent of ground I traversed in the performance of this duty was not less than thirty miles, and through this remote wilderness, I met with many parties of our own soldiers, who would have found it difficult to give a good reason for being there. Perhaps, a little farther on, some secluded hamlet showed what were the evil propensities that had brought away these marauders from the ranks of their brave comrades, for every violence that can disgrace human nature was committed by them on the defenceless inhabitants of the mountains.

In one of these small clusterings of humble dwellings, I saw three little children grouped round an object that was almost hidden by their close embrace. It was growing dark, but in so vast a solitude the sight of these tiny creatures produced an interest too strong to resist, and dismounting from my horse, I approached close to them. A bleeding corpse was the object of their infantine solicitude. A man, still young in years, lay stretched on the earth; his dark hair clotted in the stream of blood that had poured from a bayonet-wound in his breast. I looked round, every door was open, and the inmates fled. The eldest child, who at first ran away with fear at seeing me, now cautiously returned, and pointed to the door of a cottage that had been, perhaps, the happy home of his lifeless parent. I entered;—a young woman was weeping in that bitterness of anguish that knows no relief, sobs and groans choked her utterance; but I heard enough to be convinced that the knot of English marauders—for they had forfeited the name of soldiers—I had fallen in with, about a league from the spot, were the perpetrators of the horrible deed that had rendered this dwelling desolate. The exhaustion and miserable condition of the survivor gave too just a cause for apprehension that the husband had sacrificed his life in the vain effort of defending his wife from outrage.

It was midnight when I entered the village of San Pé, the head-quarters of the Commander-in-Chief and Marshal Beresford, where I found a billet allotted to me in a small farm house. A blazing fire was quickly prepared together with a good repast, for which my long ride had sharpened my appetite. In the house where I was billetted, there was an ample supply of forage for my horses and mules, nor did I scruple to apply it to their wants, as forage was at that time very difficult to obtain.

The discovery of my supply was productive of a circumstance which I relate, merely because it throws a *trait de lumière* confirmatory of the character that has so often been drawn of the Marshal, who commanded the army of Portugal. I was sitting in my room, when a Commissary dressed in all the gaudy profusion of feathers and gold lace, that distinguished that department of the Portuguese army, made his entry into the yard below, and attended by five or six peasants, proceeded without any previous communication with myself, to dismantle the granaries of their contents. I demanded by whose authority the forage was thus carried off, as I knew that by the regulations of Lord Wellington, no seizure could be made of any article without the sanction and presence of one of the municipal authorities of the commune; and in the absence of such an authority, I protested against the illegal transfer of the property.

No answer, however, was vouchsafed to my demand, and it was only upon my firm refusal to permit the seizure to take place, that my visitor withdrew, and immediately returned with a summons for me to appear instanter before his Excellency the Marshal.

Upon my arrival I was ushered into the presence of the great man, whose chafed and angry brow seemed to have gained additional height and breadth for the occasion. As he scowled upon me from the summit of his athletic form, with eyes that kindled at the opposition I had unwittingly offered to his authority, he reminded me of the picture I had often dwelt upon with terror as a child in the story of "Jack and the Ogre;" poor Jack under the bed was not in greater jeopardy than I appeared, exposed to the raging wrath of Marshal B—d.

With a voice shaking with passion, his Excellency demanded my reasons for opposing his orders, and could scarcely bear to listen to my defence, which was simply that "no municipal authority having appeared to sanction the taking of the forage, I had adhered to the regulations laid down by the Marquess of Wellington, which rendered such a proceeding essential."

"The Mayor of the Commune was in attendance upon my Commissary," thundered out the Marshal at the conclusion of the sentence.

"Pardon me, Sir," I said, "there was no municipal officer present, nor did your Commissary even mention your name as sanctioning the seizure."

"Sir," vociferated the Marshal, who had arrived at the very tip top of his constitutional thermometer, "do you mean to say I lie?—Confront the Mayor with him, and let him then deny the presence of that authority."

A movement was made towards the door, and in crept the personage, who was to confirm my guilt.

Scarcely could I preserve my gravity, as this important witness made his way through the throng of officers that surrounded the Marshal. His lean carcase was barely covered with a jacket of the coarsest texture, from the sleeves of which his elbows peeped, without, however, imparting to their owner that peculiar air of *bon ton* and independance, that is so often characteristic of a man "out at the elbows." A shirt, the original colour of which was scarcely discernible through the mass of dirt that incrusted it, was confined round his unshaven chin, by a ragged cotton handkerchief. His legs were bare, and a huge pair of wooden sabots completed the appearance of Monsieur Le Maire.

It the first time that I had trod the soil of *la belle France*, and my ideas of municipal authorities were so identified with the sleek rotundity and shining cloth which distinguish that respectable community at home, that it was with unfeigned simplicity I replied to the Marshal's impatient query of: "Now, sir, will you dispute my words?" by appealing to his Excellecy, whether he himself, unless acquainted with the fact, "would have believed that man to be a *Maire*."

It is well-known that Lord B——d was a sincere lover of a joke; indeed his propensites, in that line, obtained for him, in the 48th, the appellation of "the Joker." Whether my appeal touched some chord that vibrated agreeably in his breast; or whether reason had come to his aid, and pointed out the impossibility of my being gifted with a spirit of divination, I know not, but his Excellency was pleased to unbend his brow, and to dismiss me.

CHAPTER XVI

ST. JEAN DE LUZ

ON the 17th, head-quarters moved on to St. Jean de Luz, a populous little sea-port, twelve miles from Bayonne; here we established ourselves in the billets that had just been vacated by Marshal Soult's staff, and it might have been expected from that, and other causes, that the townspeople would have regarded us with no very friendly feeling. Such however was not the case; nor was there any reason to doubt that this outward demeanour expressed a sympathy towards us that was unfelt. The greatest attention was paid to our comforts, and after a very short residence among them, we were looked upon far more in the light of friends than invaders of their country.

One reason for this was doubtless the proclamation issued by Lord Wellington in crossing the frontier of France, to the effect that the smallest infringement on the rights and privileges of the inhabitants would be visited by punishment of the severest nature. Again, the natives of that remote part were passive spectators of the events that had sprung from the enthusiasm of the capital. The name of glory had not found its way to their mountains, and their only acquaintance with the clash of arms was derived from the passage of armed men through their peaceful vallies. On such occasions, the supplies of the country were put in requisition to maintain them. Scarcity prevailed, and the inhabitants suffered; while, on the contrary, the presence of the British troops became, through the proclamation of Lord Wellington, the guarantee of security to the inhabitants; the owners of the produce of the country received full value for it when purchased for the army, and confidence was maintained, unbroken, between the parties.

After the battle of the Nivelle, Soult had retired to the entrenched camp in front of Bayonne, extending from the Nive to the Adour. Lord Wellington pushed his advanced posts within two miles of the enemy, and in this attitude the contending armies remained for the space of one month. During the greater part of this time, the rain fell in torrents, and the road became impassable for artillery; but there was plenty of occupation in preparing bridges to cross the rivers in our front; re-equipping the guns, and replenishing the exhausted stock of the field ammunition. This work was facilitated greatly by our proximity to Passages, where the Ordnance stores were landed, and other things were landed also; to the great comfort of the officers at St. Jean de Luz.

For instance, many were the delicate patties of game and venison that came from the fair sex to their warrior Lords, with knitted purses, sashes, braces, socks, and even night-caps. The Commander-in-Chief was perhaps the least of all likely to be forgotten by his wife, in this general bazaar of love-tokens from home; and it was reported at head-quarters, that not only had the Marchioness sent out for her liege Lord's special use a plentiful supply of fleecy hosiery, but that he had liberally dispensed these treasures around him, to those whose frames were less iron-bound than his own.

So frequent was the arrival of vessels from England and Ireland during this period, that even fresh beef and vegetables found their way across the Atlantic to our tables. Upon one occasion a remarkably fine beef-steak was brought on shore at Passages by the Captain of a trader, and sent on to Sir Robert Kennedy at St. Jean de Luz with a barrel of native oysters. The steak had travelled all the way from Falmouth, and, as I afterwards found, was anxiously expected by the worthy Commissary-General, who had been apprised of its safe landing at Pasages. By some mistake the dainty morsel, and the oysters also were left at my quarters; I was out, the cook at home, and knowing that I expected friends to dinner, he naturally enough concluded that these additions to the larder were in honour of the circumstance.

Accordingly, at the appointed hour, the beef steak made its appearance, artistically served with oyster sauce, to the no small astonishment of myself and gratification of my guests, who did ample justice to its merits. The last was in the act of disappearing, when a messenger arrived from Sir Robert Kennedy, praying restitution of the delicacy, that had been left by mistake at my quarters. It is needless to say that—as in many other cases of still deeper import—the appeal was made too late to be of service to the appellant, although it does not often happen that delays are productive of as much advantage to either side as was derived by ourselves in this innocent appropriation of Sir Robert Kennedy's property.

St. Jean de Luz, after a short time, assumed all the appearance of a fashionable watering place. The breakwater that projected far into the sea, was crowded daily as a morning lounge by Lord Wellington and his brilliant staff; by the gentlemen of the Guards, and though last, not least, by many fair ladies, wives and maidens; some of whom had taken compassion on the state of celibacy to which the sons of Mars were doomed, and had arrived from England to solace them by their presence. Among these kind creatures, the Commander-in-Chief was the object of universal attention, and many a handsome "gentleman" guardsman was treated with indifference, if a look or a word from Lord Wellington was likely to be the reward. And yet, in alluding to the "gentlemen" Guards, it must be allowed that they had far more than their appearance and cognomen to boast of. Bravest of the brave in the field when called upon; they proved that neither luxurious homes nor habits can diminish in the smallest degree, the noble attributes of British manhood.

But neither "woman's smile" nor "tempter's wile" had power to wrestle from the Commander-in-Chief one moment of that watchfulness, essential to the development of those great events which were bursting into light under his auspices. His active mind did not sleep on the knowledge that an enemy—and a formidable one—lay within arm's reach; and every precaution that wisdom could adopt, and every arrangement that combination could suggest, were quietly progressing during this season of apparent rest.

St. Jean de Luz was only within a few hours ride of Passages, the depôt of our prisoners, and I determined to go over there for the purpose of ascertaining if the veteran Chasseur's son, Maurice McCarthy, was among their number.

The sun was rising in all the splendour of a sky, as I took the road to Passages, which led through the bosom of a deep ravine. On either side, the green-clad hills rose in picturesque irregularity, while here and there, a patch of cultivated land, on the steep declivities, bore witness to the industrious labour of some rustic. Nature seemed to have just doffed her night-cap, and exchanged the calm look of sleep for one of her sunniest smiles. It was one of those mornings that live in the memory; a morning, when thoughts float as lightly on the surface of the mind as gossamer threads on the light atmosphere around, when youth and spirits rush impetuously beyond the land-mark of reason, and when even age and sorrow imbibe a temporary forgetfulness of the world's cares. It was on such a morning that I bent my course towards Passages, throwing the bridle over my horse's neck, that he also might share in the happiness of nature, and forget for a while the thraldom of man's yoke. We journeyed on together, occupied with our respective thoughts, until, at the summit of a long and steep hill, Passages appeared in sight, sunk, as it were, in the depths of the earth beneath us.

There is, perhaps, no port in Europe more singularly or more romantically situated than Passages; surrounded on every side by mountains of remarkable height, the town itself stands barely raised above the level of the sea, which rolls sullenly into the basin formed by nature to receive it. The descent from the eminence on which I stood appeared terrific, and I, therefore dismounted from my horse, and tying his bridle to the projecting branch of an old tree, proceeded to reconnoitre the safest means of descending the steep road before me. A branch path interrupted the beaten track, and as the rude steps cut in the green turf denoted that it was frequented by foot travellers, I turned into it, believing that it might lead me to some public route, more adapted to my horse's powers than that in which I had left him.

The winding of the path afforded me, at each turn, a succession of varied and enchanting views. Below, perpendicularly below, was the town of Passages, reposing, as it appeared to on the bosom of the deep blue waters. The path I was pursuing became steeper and steeper; and, at a sudden bend which it took, I was led into an avenue, thickly shaded with the leaf of the umbrageous cork tree.

It appeared to lead to some habitation, for the hand of care was apparent in the paling, that protected me on one side from the yawning precipice beneath. The murmuring of a mountain brook invited me to quench my thirst in its clear waters, and as I followed mechanically the course of the little stream into which it flowed, I came unexpectedly in sight of a small chapel, round which, in rude and uncarved materials, lay the last outward signs of man's pilgrimage on earth. I advanced to take a nearer view of these quiet regions of the dead, and to contemplate the offerings that decked the graves of many. If children only were to bring their tribute of fresh flowers to deck the spot where a fond parent lies, there would be something inexpressibly touching in this association of their infantine grief, with the equally perishable emblems of their love. But the heart turns in loathing from the husband, the lover, the wife, the friend, who profanes the mystery of grief, by lifting up the veil that conceals it from the gaze of others. The act proclaims the insufficiency of the sentiment suffice to itself, which therefore seeks in action the vehemence that a state of passiveness denies. The hand that can place upon the tomb of love a flower, has never been raised to Heaven in the utter helplessness of despair. The heart that can blend one thought of verdure with the darkness of the grave, has yet to feel those depths of darkness that surround the truly wretched.

I was turning to retrace my steps, when I saw a procession slowly enter the avenue through which I had passed; on a nearer approach, I found it was composed of a military party, bearing a comrade to the burying ground in which I stood, and I fell back to witness the sad rites that were to consign a fellow being to the earth. The coffin, upon which was placed the military cap of the departed, rested upon the shoulders of four miserably clad and pallid objects, who, from their ragged apparel, I concluded to be

French prisoners. The soiled blue attire of some, who walked in mournful procession behind the coffin confirmed this supposition, and the whole party were surrounded by a detachment of our own men, who formed the escort.

The funeral convoy entered by the gate through which I had passed, and was met by a venerable priest, who issued from the ivy-grown porch of the little chapel. The service of the dead was then read, the coffin lowered down into the grave, and the party took their departure from the spot with the same decent sadness of exterior, that marked their entrance. I followed to inquire some particulars of him who had just been consigned to the silent tomb, and learnt from the sergeant of the company that the poor fellow's name was "Maurice McCarthy," that he had been desperately wounded at the battle of the Nivelle, and made prisoner at the close of the day with several others of his regiment; that every care had been taken of him, but that the agitation of his mind, in consequence of the fate of his father, who served in the same regiment—the 8th Chasseurs—had aggravated his dangerous symptoms, and that after severe suffering, he had expired on the previous day.

A bitter pang crossed my heart, as I reascended the mountain for my horse, and reflected upon the early fate of the poor fellow I had come that day to seek. To die a prisoner and alone, was in itself a fate demanding the deepest sympathy; but here was a combination of moral and physical anguish, the mind consuming the body, in the ashes of its own volcanic elements.

I led my horse down the rocky descent that led into Passages, and entered a small *posado*, which announced its reception of travellers. It was more than chilly. I ordered a fire, not meaning to return until the following day to St. Jean de Luz; and the same night, taking out of my pocket the papers confided to my charge by the dying chasseur, I perused, by the light of my lamp, the following history of a life, that reconciled me in some degree, to the fate of the young soldier whose interment I had that day witnessed.

CHAPTER XVII

AN IRISH TALE

"Heights of Zara, November, 1813.

"*To Maurice McCarthy*.

Sous-Lieutenant huitième régiment de Chasseurs.

"SHOULD these lines meet your eye, my beloved Maurice, the hand that traced them will be mouldering with the dead. Our late defeats, the strength of the pursuing army, have left us little beyond the choice of a soldier's death, or an inglorious retreat. That the first will be my fate, a mysterious presentiment assures me; and heart-rending as the task has been, I have prepared for it, by leaving to you the sad knowledge of the causes that have made us aliens to our country; and of the misery that has marked my cursed existence, and blighted the first young blossoming of yours. There is a world, my Maurice, beyond the grave! There we shall meet.

"October, 1813.

"To retrace the weary steps of time, my recollections must rest upon the one 'green spot in memory's waste'—my native land. No sooner had the long-sown seeds of tyranny and oppression burst forth into that luxuriance of blood and violence that rendered the French Revolution an unparalleled epoch in the annals of civilized nations, than the cry of liberty resounded from the shores of France, and was re-echoed through the native hills of Ireland. The sound thrilled to the heart of every lover of his country, and they were not wanting to whom the crown of martyrdom would have been welcome, to insure the liberty of Ireland. Through all ranks, the electric spark of patriotism ran, and, united in the same phalanx were to be seen the descendants of kings, and the humble peasantry of the soil. Each was alike imbued with the same grand and absorbing feeling, the deliverance of their 'fatherland' from the yoke of foreign oppression.

"It has been proved how impossible is the task of organizing and preparing a nation for active measures, against the unequal odds of awakened suspicion, treachery, counter-plots, and all the hostile array that can be produced by a stable and determined government, backed by a well-paid soldiery. In every district, select committees were appointed to represent the feelings of the mass, and as one of the leading features in the policy of the Government was to crouch in ambush, until the safe and sure moment for the annihilation of its prey, so were these committees allowed to work their own ruin by growing careless of detection.

"My father was an Irishman, but had passed his early days in England, where he had learnt to admire and cherish her institutions; venerate her religion, and appreciate her freedom. His first and best affections were blended with her name, and, on returning to his paternal inheritance in Ireland, with the wife of his love, an Englishwoman and a Protestant, he felt the sacrifice he was making of inclination to the duties to his native land.

"My only brother and myself accompanied our parents. I was the eldest, and nature had united in me all the characteristics of the people of my country. Violent and revengeful, my earliest infancy presented the fearful promise of the crimes of my manhood. Impatient of control, my pursuits led me to the haunts of the wildest characters of our neighbourhood, and surrounded by the worst associates, the evil propensities of my nature hardened into determined vice. In vain did my father warn me with all the sternness of a parent from my course of profligacy. In vain did my gentle mother, with weeping eyes, bid me for her sake renounce the errors of my ways; the demon of evil prevailed, and suffering alone was ordained to work out my repentance.

"I have mentioned that I had a brother; he was two years my junior, and beautiful in person as in mind. Oh! the agony of such a recollection as his name brings to my memory. All that I ever knew of softness then, was gazing on my brother's face; and I remember that in our days of boyhood—when, for a moment, my troubled passions found repose from exhaustion—I would hurry back to his room, and if asleep, cherish the short-lived tranquillity by bending over his innocent and placid brow. Phelim! my hand starts in tracing thy name, and my heart is turned to ice. I think I see a pale form pointing to some unknown place, as if to say, 'there we shall meet.' But why do I dwell on these phantasies of the brain, when time wanes, and I have so much to tell? Maurice, hear me to the end, and curse not my name when I am gone.

"It was in the year 1792, that I became a member of 'the Society of United Irishmen,' the nominal object of which was to cement a complete internal union of the people of Ireland to resist the weight of English influence. Treason and disaffection were universally disseminated, emissaries were sent to all parts of the kingdom by 'the United Irishmen,' to disperse seditious hand-bills through every county. In the following year, the most dreadful outrages were committed under the sacred banners of Liberty and Religion, and soon open rebellion called for the most active measures from the Government. The mass of the people were provided with pikes and bludgeons; the Protestant houses were plundered for arms, often burnt, and their inmates cruelly murdered; and such was the panic that loyal subjects deserted their homes in the disturbed counties, taking refuge in their respective county-towns, or in the metropolis.

"My frequent and prolonged absences from the paternal roof alarmed my father, who was himself, an object of suspicion, from his adherence to the cause of Loyalty and Protestantism; but I carefully avoided declaring my associations, nor even in my brother's mind, awakened the slightest distrust of my political designs.

"In the immediate neighbourhood of our home stood the cottage of my father's foster-brother, Michael O'Brien. In Ireland, this connexion is considered to bind, in bonds of the closest affection, the two beings who have drawn from the same source nature's first gift, and O'Brien's devotion to my father was of that pure and high-wrought cast which tinges the feelings of the lower Irish towards their superiors. His wife had been dead for many years, and his only child, a girl, had been brought up as the plaything of our home. Beautiful as an angel was the little Ellen O'Brien, with all the arch playfulness of Irish childhood mingled with the bashful reserve that my mother's precepts had instilled. Her disposition was like my brother's, and partook of the sweet ingenuousness of his nature. Even in her earliest days of infancy she would turn to him for refuge from the turbulent violence of my uncontrollable feelings.

"Years passed away; the boys were transformed to men, and the little Ellen to a lovely woman. It was on my return from college, where my untutored mind had grovelled low in profligacy and vice, that the natural beauty of Ellen O'Brien met my enraptured gaze. I had never, in fancy's wildest dream, seen a form so exquisitely bright, and the admiration I attempted not to conceal, was received with that careless indifference that rendered her still more captivating in my sight. With a feeling of wild jealousy, I turned to my brother's countenance, expecting to see in it the reflection of those feelings that had rushed with overwhelming force through my being. It wore the calmness that was its peculiar character, and his eye, beaming with tender affection, rested alternately on Ellen and myself.

"I turned away, never to know peace again; one all-absorbing passion held me fast, and cursed me. Oh! the agony that followed! for mine was not a fancy to be wafted from the mind by the first passing breeze of novelty, but I was doomed to suffer and to feel alone. No kindred flame lighted up the beautiful cheek of Ellen. She heard me, pitied me, and spurned me.

"From that day existence became a weight from which I laboured to escape, and every dark feeling of my mind blackened into hatred of my fellow-creatures. On the same day that the cup of happiness had been dashed for ever from my lips, I met my brother. I would have hurried past him, but he stopped me, and as our eyes met, I saw in his an expression of tender sadness that I did not then understand. Oh! why did I ever learn its import?

I saw Ellen no more. She was removed from the home of her childhood, and I concluded that, by her own wish, she had been placed beyond the power of my importunities. Vainly did I seek her, and maddened by the force of contending feelings, I plunged deeply into the agitated ocean of revolution, and became a traitor and a rebel.

"During the years 1794 and 1795, rebellion had risen to the most fearful height, and it was found impossible to allay the spirit of outrage that actuated the people. 'The united Irishmen' were in the foremost ranks of the rebellion, and their activity succeeded, in many instances, in seducing the military from their allegiance. To this society—destined as I madly thought to regenerate Ireland—I was bound hand and heart, and hailed with frantic joy the approaching crisis that was to sever the bonds that united her to England. The whole county of Cork was in open insurrection; yet still my father, with all the determination that was shown at that period, by numbers of the Irish gentry, refused to quit the home of his ancestors, and prepared to defend, to the last extremity, his property against invaders. Little did he think that his elder son was destined to be the destroyer of his race— the blood-hound to track the prey! A meeting was convened of delegates from the many secret committees throughout the country, and I received a summons to attend as agent to 'The united Irishmen.'

"The rendezvous was given in the subterranean passage of the old monastery; some parts of the building were still standing, while rude masses of stone, heaped under the mouldering walls, gave evidence of the ruin that time had wrought upon the rest. The road leading to this remote spot was wild and lonely; and the chill air of a November evening breathed through the murky atmosphere. I wrapped around me my cloak, which bore the badge of our confederacy, and impatient from excitement, traversed the dark and silent plains. While thus advancing, the fog seemed to gather round me, and the path I had taken was no longer discernible. I hesitated whether to proceed, when a feeble light from afar awakened my attention. It was in the direction of the monastery, and from its elevation might almost have been mistaken for a star emerging from the denseness of the fog; but upon a near approach, the rays became more vivid, and falling on the objects beneath, enabled me to ascertain that they proceeded from an aperture in that part of the monastery, which had escaped, in some degree, the ravages of time.

"That we were betrayed, was the first idea that presented itself to my mind, and I hurried onwards to apprize my confederates of their danger, and to disperse them, if possible, before it was too late. With hasty steps, I traversed the uneven ground, where prostrate pillars and broken arches told of former splendour. All was silent as the tomb; and it was only as I wended down the stone stairs that led to the vault, wherein treason was to hold her vigils, that I remembered how my impatience had anticipated the hour of meeting, and that I had some anxious moments to pass before the arrival of my confederates. Cautiously I groped my way back to the open air, and still the same light, issuing from the turret above me, excited my surprise. Mounting on a projecting part of the edifice, that was thickly covered by a luxuriant ivy tree, I discovered an outer staircase that led apparently to that part of the building from whence the mysterious light proceeded.

"With difficulty I extricated my feet from the creeping plants that concealed it from view, and as I slowly moved upwards, a voice riveted me to the spot where I stood. 'Phelim,' it gently uttered, 'do not engage yourself against such desperate men, for my sake, for our boy's sake, give up your intention to denounce them to the Government. Who will protect your Ellen and her child, if, in these dangerous times, you exchange your peaceful home for the violence of civil war.'

"My brain grew dizzy as I listened. It was Ellen—the Ellen of my ardent love who spoke. I advanced, with frantic impatience to the aperture, where still flickered the light that had so fatally allured me. My eyes rested on a scene that maddened my senses to delirium. On Ellen's knees rested the head of Phelim—my brother—her eyes were fixed on his with all the fond expression of reproach, that fear for the safety of a loved being can infuse, while at the same time her foot rocked, at measured intervals, the cradle of her first-born—the child of Phelim.

"Feelings of the darkest rage boiled in my breast, and my heart heaved with the hope of being justified in an act of vengeance by the answer I should hear. Its pulses beat quick and loud, and vainly I strived to calm its rioting, so that I might hearken to what the enemy of our cause would say. His words fell low, and hesitatingly. My name, suspicion, rebel, fell like molten lead on the fibres of my brain; a low whistle sounded from beneath, I bounded to the signal, and that night planned my hellish scheme of vengeance.

"Important intelligence had been communicated from Dublin of the successful demonstrations of the partizans of liberty; and in every county it was expected that similar proofs would be given of zealous adherence to the one great cause. A general attack was ordered to be made upon the Protestant landholders, and even upon those suspected of harbouring political opinions opposed to the reigning democracy.

"Twenty-four hours had scarcely passed away since the meeting of the delegates at the monastery, when an armed force, composed of the most desperate of the country, was placed at my disposal for the execution of the previous night's project. Among the obnoxious was my aged father; but he had, by a life of unfeigned benevolence and good-will towards his neighbours, inspired even the depredators with a sentiment of respect. To obtain fire-arms was the grand object of the rebels, and as he was known to have prepared himself for resistance, it was proposed that his house should be first visited—not for the object of plunder—but to take possession of the weapons that were supposed to be concealed.

"Night had no sooner covered the earth, and prepared it for dark deeds, than we sallied forth, two hundred men strong, under the banner of 'Liberty or death.' The remembrance of that night appals my mind with horror. Oh! that I could blot it out from the page of life!

"My father made a resistance worthy of his noble bearing; inch by inch, he, and his faithful servants disputed the violation of the domestic hearth; but numbers prevailed, and as the ruffians rushed impetuously onwards, inflamed by the opposition they encountered, I vainly endeavoured to check the violence of their progress. At the moment that the first report of fire arms announced the commencement of a sanguinary conflict, the sound of a trumpet burst on our ears, and a body of cavalry advancing into the court-yard dashed with fury upon the assailants. The attack was as vigorously repulsed, until the very floors of the apartments streamed with blood; and pierced with bullets, the devoted Michael O'Brien fell on the body of his master, whom he had vainly to save!

"The rebels defended themselves with desperation against the military, shouting, as an incentive to their violence, the name of 'Phelim McCarthy.' The superiority, however, of the soldiers prevailed, and the issue of the conflict was no longer doubtful; when a tremendous cheer burst from the direction of the road, and a large force of well-organized and well-armed men appeared on the scene of action. The discouraged band of rebels rallied at the well-known cry, and with fresh vigour, joined in the slaughter of the English foe. Night was far advanced when the work of blood was over, and the victorious rebels, led on by myself, advanced, flushed with success, to the monastery.

"The moon had just risen, and was shedding her first pale rays over the turret that contained the objects, both of my fiercest hatred, and most passionate love. I enjoined silence to the infuriated rabble, who were thirsting for the blood of the informer, and advanced alone to the staircase, to which my dark destiny led me on the preceding night. Ascending rapidly, I stood once more on that spot, where first I marked my victims. Once more I gazed upon the face of Ellen; she was asleep, and the light of the rising moon played on that sweet countenance that lay nestled in the bosom of Phelim. My heart turned to gall at the sight. I sprang from the aperture to the wall beneath, and cheered on my followers. A dense smoke rose in columns round the turret, and one blaze of fire soon pointed, in thousands of spiral forms, to the great canopy of Heaven. The fresh breeze of night, for a moment, separated the flames, and, in that momentary glance, I saw—oh, God! my brother vainly endeavouring, with one arm, to place his child beyond the power of the flames, while with the other he closely pressed Ellen to his heart. My brain grew mad. I rushed through the burning element—from stone to stone I leapt, till the blazing woodwork stopped my further progress; yet still I braved its fury, and reached the aperture.

"'My brother,' he exclaimed.

"'Thy murderer,' I shrieked. Oh! once before I had seen the same sad, yet soft, look with which now he gazed upon me, the last that ever beamed from that beautiful eye.

"A report like thunder echoed through the lofty arches, and as I still clung, in madness, to tottering wall, my brother with one desperate effort placed within my grasp his child! At the same moment, the whole edifice fell in one mass of smouldering ruins. How I escaped, I know not, for weeks passed away, and I retained no recollection of that night of crime. I know that a woman nursed me into life, and gave a mother's care to the sweet boy of Phelim and Ellen—that I fostered him, loved him, have lived for him, and on the battlefield have encountered death for him. If in these last few lines, my Maurice, you recognise some faint outline of my love for you, let that love guide your remembrance of me when I am gone. Think of me as I have been to you, the fond father, the faithful friend. One who has endeavoured to cherish in you the virtues you received from your parents; and to instil into your young mind abhorrence of the violent passions that have agitated my stormy life. Farewell! there is a world beyond the grave. Phelim—Ellen—Maurice, THERE WE SHALL MEET."

The church bell struck the hour of midnight, and roused me from the reverie into which I had been plunged by the contents of the papers before me. I replaced them in my pocket, in the hope that, by one of those strange fatalities that issue from the wheel of chance, I might be brought into contact with those to whom they might be of interest. I retired to bed, but not to rest, my disturbed spirit was haunted by image of love, sorrow, crime, in fearful array, the offspring of my evening's occupation, and I felt glad when the dawn of morning broke upon the darkness of my chamber, and in some degree dispelled the thoughts that had driven sleep from my eyelids. I hastily rose, and ordering my horse, retraced my steps to St. Jean de Luz.

CHAPTER XVIII

FIVE DAYS OF FIGHTING

THE first outbreak that took place between the hostile armies was on the 9th of December, when the divisions under Beresford and Hill drove the French from their advanced posts on the Nive, while Sir John Hope, with the left wing of the army moving from St. Jean de Luz, attacked the posts in front of their entrenched camp, and forced them to retire within its lines.

In the early part of the day, a curious incident occurred to relieve the monotony of hard blows. At a short distance from the high road leading to Bayonne was the Château Anglet, the property of a French gentleman, whose confidence in the strength of the French army had blinded his eyes to the possibility of its defeat. In conjunction with this ill-timed security, every thing was left in the château as might have been expected in a time of profound peace; and the owner had the happiness, moreover, of exercising both his patriotism and hospitality in favour of General Villatte, who, with his staff, occupied the château as *quartier-général*; with so efficient a garrison, away with fears for the safety of the fortress!

On the route of our troops from St. Jean de Luz, the skirmishing had been very sharp within a mile of the château, which was in itself an object, when once espied, not likely to be passed by without a closer acquaintance with it. The flank companies of the 4th regiment having approached, under cover of the hedges, close to the rear of the mansion, made a rushing entrance at the back; while at the same moment a numerous party of French staff-officers fled precipitately from the front door to the gate where their horses stood in readiness. So great was their flurry and confusion that some had left their hats behind them—others their swords.

They had evidently been surprised, and as it turned out, at a moment that must have been particularly *mal à propos*, as the intruders found an excellent *déjeûner a la fourchette* prepared for the General, who had snatched from glory a few leisure moments to invigorate the outward man. Chickens, cutlets, and other delicacies were pounced upon with no gentle avidity by the hungry soldiers; nor could the strict orders that had been issued by Lord Wellington, prevent the transfer from the table to the pocket, of every silver spoon and fork within reach. Nor did they stop there, for the château was rifled from top to bottom of every valuable and portable article, in an incredibly short space of time.

An hour afterwards I saw a corporal of the 4th regiment lying dead under a hedge. A crimson damask cushion supported his head, whether the luxurious booty was carried off by himself, or placed there by some friendly hand, I was unable to determine.

The 10th was a day of severe fighting, for Soult tried hard to recover his lost position, but was opposed by Sir John Hope, whose valorous bearing on the field was most conspicuous. The result of the conflict was the complete defeat of the enemy.

The fighting of the next two days was attended with similar success to the allies, and on the 13th, Soult, driven to desperation by such continued failures, passed through Bayonne in the night, and burst with all his strength upon Hill's corps, in the hope of breaking through the position of the allied army. The struggle was tremendous, and more than once the success of the day fearfully doubtful. The troops, on both sides, fought with a vigour that had perhaps never been surpassed; but the indomitable front presented by some of the British regiments, turned again and again the tide of fortune in their favour. During many hours, Hill's corps, consisting of less than eighteen thousand men, bore the brunt of an engagement with forty thousand of the enemy, and although the French were seen to give way at several points, at others they still retained sufficient strength to continue the conflict.

Positions were taken and retaken at the point of the bayonet. The 92nd, under the gallant veteran Cameron, was at one time nearly overwhelmed by the force of numbers, and obliged to give way; but it was only for a moment; again reforming their skeleton ranks, they returned to the charge with bagpipes playing and colours flying, led on by their Colonel, sword in hand, over the bodies of their slain comrades.

With a shout that rose above the shrill tones of the pipes, the veterans charged, in ranks two deep, the mass before them, and regained the up-land ground they had lost. Such noble efforts were not made in vain. At every point the enemy gave way, and the sixth division coming up with Lord Wellington in person, was just in time to render still more decisive the victory that Hill had already won. Closely pursued by the allies, the French Marshal retreated with the greater part of his army to the Adour, leaving a garrison of ten thousand men for the defence of Bayonne.

The heroism displayed on both sides during these five days' fighting was not confined to the action of hostility between man and man. Patience, under the severest trials, formed no inconsiderable feature of it. To march over roads knee-deep in mud, to lie exposed, during inclement nights, to pouring rain, were evils in themselves almost sufficient to damp the glowing ardour of enterprise; but it was not so. Animated with the generous spirit of comradeship in dangers and privations, the officers did not point out the way of bearing them, but in their own persons showed how they were to be borne, and the soldiers nobly followed in the wake of such glorious examples.

It may almost be doubted, much as the mind dwells with enthusiasm on the deeds of brave men, whether the reckless exposure to which Sir John Hope subjected himself, was not carried to an extent that wisdom might censure as inexcusable in a General, on whom rested the responsibility of directing movements in the field. Be that as it may, nothing can deteriorate from the splendid parade of gallantry his warlike figure presented, moving wherever the fight was thickest, cheering and encouraging the troops. The pen of a Napier has rescued from the oblivion of time many names that threw a lustre over the battle of the Nive, and it is to be lamented that modesty did not permit that historian to record that the veterans of the 43rd were led on by himself to the glorious distinction they obtained. As long as chivalrous bravery is honoured and esteemed, such men as Beresford, Hill, Kempt, Barnard, Colborne, Pringle, Barnes, Cameron, and many others, will shed an unfading splendour upon generations yet unborn, through the genius of that brother hero. The result of these five days' fighting, which cost the French upwards of six thousand, and the allies five thousand men, gave to Lord Wellington the free and undisturbed possession of the country extending from the Pyrenees to the Adour, thus laying bare before his victorious army, the southern plains of France.

CHAPTER XIX

A SAD STORY

AFTER the battle of the Nive, St. Jean de Luz again assumed its jaunty appearance as head-quarters of the army. The breakwater again thronged, and many amateurs arrived from England to learn the art of war in snug quarters. Some few came also from the holier and dearer motive of gazing once again on those whom the fortune of war had spared throughout the perils and dangers of so many battlefields; while others again were drawn to St. Jean de Luz in the hope of solacing, by their presence, some beloved relative, who was perhaps slowly recovering from wounds received at the battle of the Nive.

Among these sufferers was a youth too interesting, both from his merits and early fate, to be forgotten. The short life of this gallant boy had been full of romantic incident and change of fortune, and was recounted to me by one who had watched it from its earliest dawn.

His father, the only son of a wealthy Yorkshire Squire, brought up with every indulgence that could tend to weaken the powers of self-denial, and strengthen the natural inclination of youth to the indulgence of the passions, had formed, in early life, an attachment to the daughter of his father's gamekeeper. Such intimacies are more difficult to conceal in the midst of village gossips, than in the populous districts of large towns, and reports were soon spread far and wide, sadly prejudicial to the pure fame of the country girl.

The Squire heard the rumours, and merely tracing in them some fleeting cause for the frequent absences of his son from home, determined to plead in favour of a reputation, which had hitherto been spotless among the village maidens. His task was, however, anticipated by one who had watched with anxiety, increasing to agony, the altered mien of a beloved child; and on the same day that the proud Squire proposed cautioning his heir against an intimacy that would also diminish his importance in the neighbourhood, the aged gamekeeper boldly, but with a breaking heart, came to the Hall to demand, as man from man, the only atonement that could be made for the seduction of his innocent child.

With a light and joyous step, the young man bounded into his father's study at the moment when the tear of insulted feeling and honest indignation stood unwiped in the eye of the old faithful servant. "He had lived too long," he said, "to hear his Mary's honour bartered for with gold."

The young man's brow glowed with the flush of generous warmth as he grasped the shrivelled hand that would have recoiled, as if from a serpent's touch: "Nay, hear me," he exclaimed, while for a moment his eye rested on the incensed countenance of his father. "My errand here was to proclaim the truth, and openly avow that your dear Mary," turning to the aged gamekeeper, "has been for three months past, my lawful wife."

Some years had elapsed since the event we have just recorded. The Squire had dragged on a cheerless and desolate existence; the son of his affections had been sacrificed to wounded pride, and in a distant part was earning, by the sweat of his brow, the daily maintenance of himself and Mary. The old gamekeeper lay in the church-yard close by, and the sweet boy that often stole away to deck the old man's grave with flowers, had never even heard of another grandsire than he, so loved and honoured by the cottage group.

But even this chequered happiness was to find an end. The once strong health of Mary's faithful guardian and protector gave way; his cheek grew pale, and his frame each day looked more and more attenuated; the daily bread became more sparing, and at last, poverty in its heaviest form weighed on the once happy inmates of the cottage.

Under this prostration of misery and helplessness, poor Mary resolved to make known her husband's declining state of health to his father. Their first advances for forgiveness had been met with resolute denial; but time is a crucible, by which men's hearts are tested with unerring truth and few there are who do not either lose qualities, or gain them, in the process. The father's had undergone a change; affection yearned for the blessing that even pride but faintly opposed; and the dying son was again restored to the scenes of his early youth, and perilous first love.

But death's shaft had sped; nor the delight of renewed affection, nor gratitude for the delicate attentions lavished on Mary and his boy, could arrest its progress. He died some weeks after his return to the parental roof, and felt there was no need of recommending his loved wife and child to the kindness of his father.

If affection can be transferred from one object to another with an increase of force to what we love the last, it was so in the case of this bereaved father and the little Henry. Years wore away; the grieving Mary had found a rest from sorrow by her husband's side, and the little cottage urchin was now the Eton boy, and grandsire's heir. It is rare, indeed, that we are not made to feel sooner or later the penalty of former errors, even though it should reach us through ramifications that seem to have no connexion with them.

Like Norval of old, the youth had heard of battles, and his young heart beat high to earn a name beyond the dull sounding one of a country Squire. In vain the doating grandfather used first persuasion, then argument, then force. The proud boy spurned the latter, and stealing clandestinely from the gates that had been closed in anger upon his father, proceeded to London on foot, and offered himself as a volunteer in the — regiment, then under orders for the Peninsula. His youth and appearance soon brought forth a disclosure of the truth, and after some necessary negotiations between the Colonel and the grandfather, the latter acceded to the wishes of the lad, and he was Gazetted to an ensigncy in the regiment.

From that moment, the young soldier's life was one brilliant, but alas! too short a career of intrepidity and gallantry. At Salamanca,

Fuentes d'Onore, Vittoria, and the Pyrenees, the steady bravery of his youthful figure, leading to the charge a band of veterans, drew the burst of applause and thrill of admiration from the sternest breasts. Susceptible as nature's gentlest child to every vibration of love and tenderness, he was equally an adept, by nature's art, in the most delicate intricacies of the path of honour. Ready to take and to return the harmless joke, or happy jest, bold would have been the man who sought for more, at the expense of the high-spirited young Ensign.

With such excellences of mind, combined with almost perfection of person, can it be wondered at, that, after the battle of the Nive, when the serjeant of the company to which he belonged, brought him into St. Jean de Luz badly wounded in that breast, that had never yet palpitated but with sentiments of virtue and of honour, tears ran fast from eyes unaccustomed to weeping, and that but one deep settled gloom followed the announcement of the intelligence to all who knew him? It was some weeks after the battle of the Nive before I again saw the youthful warrior. The first warm rays of an early southern spring had brought him from his quarters to breathe the invigorating air. But he was not alone: a man, bent down with care more than by age, sustained the weak and tottering steps of the youth. The pale cheek of the once robust young soldier was spotted in the centre with a hectic flush that foretold the early tomb: that spoke of high-wrought feelings brought into flower too soon to blossom long. Each day I saw them thus—the grandsire and the grandson—but one day I missed them, although the sun shone bright gaily. I called to inquire the cause, and found that this lovely bud of chivalry and honour had drooped to its parent earth.

The grandfather was left alone. A few days afterwands, I saw him at Passages, and it seemed as if a century of time and suffering had settled on his lofty brow since last we met. I stood upon the shore, gazing on the receding vessel that was carrying back to England this last of an honoured race. He stood upon the deck, one hand placed on his bursting heart, the other extended over the black pall that covered the remains of his beloved grandchild, as if to shelter him still from the storms of this world.

CHAPTER XX

SPANISH OUTRAGES

DURING the lull of hostilities after the battle of the Nive, our advanced posts, and those of the enemy were within short distances of each other, without either party suffering the smallest annoyance from the proximity. Sentries were relieved, and patrols went their prescribed rounds, frequently exchanging courtesies and kindly words.

Not so with the Spaniards. Murillo's troops, encouraged by himself to look on France as the land of promise, on which might be wreaked the full debt of vengeance owed by Spain, made frequent inroads across the frontier, plundering the inhabitants and committing the most wanton atrocities on the defenceless. Lord Wellington's judicious proclamation was treated with disregard by all the Spanish Generals, Mina himself being nothing backward in exciting his troops to rapine and plunder. The Basque provinces were in arms to repel the aggressive violence, and Soult ably took advantage of this emanation of indignation to excite them to a mountain warfare that would have aided, in no small measure, his own views.

A few days before the termination of this eventful year, I was surprized by a visit from my former host, the Padre of Vera. I had often thought of him, and not less frequently on the scene I had witnessed in his mountain-home, on the night before we parted. The good man was sadly changed, and his once tranquil countenance wore an anxious, excited expression, that strongly reminded me of his sister.

Glad of the opportunity of requiting some portion of the hospitality he had shown me, I prevailed on him to become my guest for a few days; and in that brief space, I became initiated into the knowledge of some of the atrocities that had been committed by Murillo's troops; atrocities that were never even heard of at the head-quarters of Lord Wellington, and that could only find issue to the light of day through such channels as that which brought them to my knowledge.

It was long before I could bring myself to ask tidings of Agnese, and even then, before there was time for an answer, the name of the Friar Antonio escaped my lips in the same breath. The Padre looked up, as if surprised to hear from me the combination of those names, and a flush of crimson dye overspread his usually pallid countenance. "Name him not," he passionately exclaimed, as, for a moment the incensed feelings of frail mortality rose with resistless force above the habitual subjection of the spirit. "Name him not, the accursed!" With this vehement injective seemed to have exhaled, in some degree, the poor Padre's ebullition of wrath, and crossing himself with lowly reverence, he effected the mastery of his feelings sufficiently to acquaint me with the following circumstances.

After the battle of the Nive, Murillo's Spanish division was placed in cantonments on the mountain heights. Under the pretence of scanty provisions, these lawless marauders invaded the surrounding villages, committing murders, and other revolting crimes on the defenceless people who inhabited those secluded regions. The Convent of St. Cecilia, situated within the valley of Bastan, offered an allurement to the wild passions of such men as these; and their General himself, the blood-thirsty, savage-hearted Murillo, was more ready to lead on to crime, than to oppose his authority to check it. To this convent then, a fierce horde of Spanish soldiers repaired at an hour of darkness well suited to the guilt that was to be consummated.

The difficulty of gaining ingress to the building was an obstacle to be overcome by one, who held within the walls a sway, that had been already subservient to the ruin of many a wretched inmate. That impious guide to the brute passions of the Spanish soldiers was no other than the friar Antonio. But this monster of human iniquity had yet his price, for which he had bartered woman's life, and woman's honour. There was one fair girl in the convent, who had been the friend in childhood of the lost Agnese; like the latter, she had become the object of the licentious friar's wishes, but unlike her friend, had repelled with loathing his repeated attempts to undermine her virtue.

Determined, at all risks, to possess the object of his unholy thoughts, Antonio entered into a league with Murillo's troop of ruffians, and disguised as one of them, led the way, through the darkness of the night, to the convent.

In the mean time, Agnese, during a lengthened visit to the convent, had received the confidence of her youthful friend, and listened with feelings of distracted jealousy and indignation to a recital of the faithlessness of him she had loved with so much peril to her soul. Maddened with contending passions, Agnese took the determination of unfolding to her brother her own lost condition, demanding from him vengeance on the head of the guilty Antonio, and permission to seek the forgiveness of Heaven by a life of penitence in the Convent of St. Cecilia.

The Padre's feelings must have been terrible at the disclosure, to judge by the violent paroxysm of emotion the recital of it produced. The habitual serenity of his nature had given way beneath the shock, and where only gentleness had breathed before, was now perceptible no small measure of the Spaniard's violence, and unextinguishable feelings of revenge.

In these latter feelings, however, his unfortunate sister had no share. Her still tender years, and apparent contrition, while pleading in her favour, only added to the fire of hatred that burned fiercely in his breast against Antonio; and at the same time that schemes of revenge that might bring to retributive justice the wily liar floated in his thoughts, he listened with patient forbearance to the tale of guilt his sister had to tell, and warmly acquiesced in the sacrifice she contemplated of her young life to the expiation of her sin.

On the night of that same day which saw the penitent Agnese received by the Abbess and sisterhood into the convent of St.

Cecilia, a body of armed men, guided by the villain Antonio, descended from the mountains to the peaceful valley, through which the convent-bell was sounding for the hour of prayer. The friar's cowl was quickly thrown over the military garb he had assumed, as the ruthless band stole with stealthy steps to the front entrance of the building.

With meek and holy accents the friar claimed admittance of the porter from within, an aged man, to whom his voice was known, and who had orders to admit the reverend brother on his sacred missions to the sisterhood. As the ponderous iron gate opened slowly to admit this rare specimen of Satan's workmanship, the soldiers burst from behind into the lofty hall that led to the cloisters of the women. The friar had disappeared, and in his stead a tall athletic soldier, more demoniacal in purpose, more relentless in execution than the rest, led the way to the chapel, where the intended victims were engaged in prayer. Over the scene that followed time has not even yet thrown the shadow of oblivion, for it remains to this day a tale of horror for the winter's hearth, remembered by many an aged native of the Pyrenees. None of those helpless women escaped the brutal violence of Murillo's soldiers. The convent was set on fire in many places, and when the peasants from the neighbouring mountains, attracted by the flames, repaired to the scene of rapine, they found the edifice a burning mass of ruins.

Among the few who rushed in the wildness of despair through the devouring element was Agnese; the wretched girl had recognised in the foremost of that ruffian band, the demon Friar—had shrieked his name again and again, until the vaulted ceiling echoed with it, and received his stab of vengeance in the bosom where his image was too faithfully enshrined.

Still preserving consciousness through the terrors that surrounded her, the unfortunate Agnese sprung, when all was over, through the smoke that densely closed upon the appalling scene, and gaining strength by despair, cleared the burning timbers, and found refuge in the open space of the court-yard. It was here that the mountaineers had assembled, and here that they discovered the bleeding and apparently lifeless form of the Padre's sister. They raised her from the earth, and bore her to her mountain home at Vera, where, in her brother's arms, she finished her miserable existence.

CHAPTER XXI

THE INVESTMENT OF BAYONNE

THE glorious campaign of 1813 received its last laurel by the victory of the Nive, which completed the triumph of that eventful year.

The head-quarters of the army were still at St. Jean de Luz, where Lord Wellington awaited the result of negotiations then pending between the foreign powers of Europe and Napoleon, and upon which results depended the advance of the army under his command upon the territory of France.

In the meanwhile, the French loyalist party began to show itself more openly, in consequence of the despondency into which the retreat from Moscow had thrown the partisans of Napoleon. Adversity and failure are the tests of popularity, and the sanguine temperament of the French nation could ill brook the change from glorious conquest to ignoble defeat.

The spell of invincibility attached to Napoleon's name was broken, and with it fell the enthusiasm that had sprung from it. For the first time, it was discovered that the strength of the nation had been squandered in pursuit of the chimerical visions of ambition; that the blood of hundreds of thousands had been sacrificed to the aggrandizement of the few. These late discoveries, originating in the adverse circumstances that had placed an impassable barrier to Napoleon's onward course, had the effect of multiplying the difficulties of his position.

The Royalists, on the one side, were no less zealous to restore to legitimacy its rights, than the Ultra-Republicans to destroy an individual despotism, that had not even the tinsel mantle of glory to conceal it. Between these two extreme parties, stood another, far more numerous, whose members were characterized, some by indifference, others by love of change.

With an eye of scrutiny, Europe looked on the contending elements thus bound up in the French nation, and terms of peace were placed at a proportionately greater distance from its rulers' grasp.

While thus awaiting the signal "to march, or not to march," St. Jean de Luz was as gay and agreeable as ever; dinners, soirées, and balls beguiled the time, and sutlers swarmed like flies on a summer's day, in the well-founded hope of making cent per cent by their champagne and claret. Even hock found its way from the "Banks of the Rhine" into the possession of these gentlemen venders, who sold it for a "consideration."

The time thus sped merrily along; and Christmas-day was not only hailed with as much fun and frolic as could have welcomed it in England, but roast beef and plum-pudding lent their aid to the illusion that we were, *de facto*, at home. Hospitality and conviviality went hand-in-hand; of the latter, some judgment may be formed by the regulation adopted to disperse the guests, which movement was only to take place when the empty champagne bottles met in the centre of a long dinner-table, forming an uninterrupted line of communication between the President and Vice-President.

The life and joy of these joyous parties was Captain Moray, aide-de-camp to the Quarter-Master-General, and beloved by every one as perhaps no other was. Young, handsome, brave, gentle, and ingenuous, this officer was the centre, round whom all others gathered. The very sound of his laugh was catching; and many a sour face was irresistibly led into a smile by its contagious harmony.

We arranged a rendezvous one evening at Fontarabia, a little town between St. Jean de Luz, and Passages, which afforded quarters to some of the officers; among others, to two of my earliest friends, Colonels Nichol, and William Mein, the former commanding the 43rd, the latter the 52nd regiments. To these gallant brothers, the honour of our visit was intended; accordingly, we sallied forth on a very ugly night on our expedition. It was so dark, that at first we only advanced our horses at a snail's pace, which neither accommodating our appetites nor high spirits, these last got the better of prudence, and we started off pretty briskly, reckless of the consequences.

As thus we pushed along, my horse, which was upon the off side, plunged with his two forelegs into the centre of a wet ditch, and having deposited me therein, almost up to my neck in water, scrambled out on the opposite side, and pursued his way rejoicing at his loss. The loud halloo that I gave was the only indication my companions received of our having parted company on the road; and when they at length returned, guided by the sound of my voice to the spot of my immersion, we all laughed so immoderately that a considerable time elapsed before I could make the necessary exertions to relieve myself from the unpleasant position. When this was effected, I had no alternative but to mount *en croupe* behind one of the party; for my steed had not been sufficiently complaisant to proffer his assistance, and thus we journeyed on to Fontarabia.

We found our gallant hosts in excellent quarters, at the house of a French family, where they were looked upon, to use their own phrase as "*les enfans de la maison;*" and surely if gentleness, simplicity, and truth, are qualities that inspire affection everywhere, none could deserve a larger share of it than Colonel William Mein of the 52nd.

This officer entered the service at a very early age, as a subaltern in the 52nd, and served with that distinguished regiment through all the campaigns of the Peninsula. At the storming of Ciudad Rodrigo, he fell severely wounded while leading on to the attack, the Grenadier company of his regiment. Still suffering from the effects of his wounds, he rejoined it the day preceding the assault of Badajoz, and his re-appearance among the veterans of the 52nd afforded a genuine testimony of his worth, for the whole regiment turned out to welcome him with three ringing cheers. On the following night, he led his company to the attack, and was struck down amidst heaps of slain, where he lay without signs of life, until a friendly hand removed him from the scene of carnage.

The spirit of chivalry that burned in the hearts of the men of the light division, effected a quicker cure to their wounds than did the Leech's skill, and it was not long before the gallant soldier again appeared at the head of the regiment on the hills of the Bidassoa; and though severely wounded, continued to follow, at that signal victory, in the pursuit of the enemy, until fainting from exhaustion, he was carried to the rear.

The battle of the Nive was the last scene of strife in which this brave man took a part. Shot through the neck and shoulder on the second day's fighting, he was taken to Fontarabia, and was slowly recovering under the skilful and kind care of Dr. Gunning, Surgeon to the forces, at the time that we bethought ourselves of enlivening his retirement.

On arriving, I found that my horse had preceded me, and was put up in better quarters than his desertion merited. My wet clothes were exchanged for others, raised by general subscription, and we sat down to a dinner, which, owing to the good purveyorship of the sutlers, was prolonged to a later hour than was consistent with the still weak condition of our brave host.

In the beginning of February, the allied army renewed hostilities by forcing the enemy to withdraw from the right of the Adour, while Sir John Hope prepared to cross that river below Bayonne. For this purpose, a bridge of rare and laborious construction, which had been planned by Colonel Sturgeon and completed by the Staff Corps, was held in readiness to be thrown over the Adour when required.

A battalion of the guards, by means of pontoon boats, had crossed the river about two miles below the fortress of Bayonne, under cover of a battery of six eighteen pounders, commanded by Captain Morrison, and a rocket troop under the command of Captain Lane. The rockets showed less of disobedience than had been their wont at many previous experimental trials on Woolwich Marsh, preserving the straight line of duty prescribed to them, in spite of all prognostics to the contrary.

A firm footing being thus established on the right bank of the river, the bridge that had been prepared, was ordered to be thrown across, to effect which, a certain number of *chasse-marées* were sent round the coast from Passages laden with anchors, and other essentials for the foundation. The bridge itself was to be supported by the *chasse-marées*, securely anchored at equal distances across the river.

The entrance of the Adour was at all times attended with peril to craft of every description, owing to a bar of sand, over which the waves, in boisterous weather, rolled with fearful violance. On the day when the *chasse-marées* appeared at the mouth of the river, bearing the materials for the formation of the bridge, a high wind had driven a tempestuous sea over the bar, raising a mountain of surf that seemed to defy the approach of the little flotilla, that gallantly pressed forward, led by the boats of our men of war.

Having been one of the many who watched from the shore, with anxious heart, the progress of the operation, I can bear testimony to the dauntless courage of those to whom its execution was confided. The first to lead the way through the uncertain channel of the river—for the enemy had removed the buoys that marked it—was O'Reilly, the same who commanded the sailors' battery at St. Sebastian.

For a moment the boat held on, while he paused for some indication that might guide him in the course to take. During that momentary pause, which showed him nothing but the raging surf, he turned to his brave companion, Captain Faddy of the artillery, who had voluntarily accompanied him, and in a low voice told him to unbuckle his sword—a precaution he had himself taken, and which, in human parlance, saved the lives of both.

The moment's pause was over; the order "Give way, my lads," was uttered, and through the giant surf the cutter dashed, now carried to a fearful height on the summit of the waves—now borne with irresistible fury, crashing on the shore, overwhelmed by the burst of waters. The sight was appalling. Arms were stretched out from shore, as if available to save, and almost miraculously as it appeared, they were destined to do so. O'Reilly was thrown senseless on the sands, and before the rushing surge could reclaim its victim, the soldiers had linked their hands in one strong line, and running into the turbulent waters, had borne him from his perilous position. Faddy, unencumbered by his sword, had managed to swim to shore, as did also some of the crew; the rest were drowned.

Upon seeing the disastrous occurrence, the Spanish crews held back, and it was only when the wind was considerably lulled, that the attempts were renewed to cross the bar. Even then, a fine young officer of the Lyra sloop of war perished with the whole of his boat's crew. Many other valuable lives were lost; and it was left for an agent of transports, Mr. Debenham, to achieve what the most heroic efforts had failed in doing; his small boat leaping, as it may be said, over the boiling surge, in safety on the shore. The *chasse-marées* followed in the line, and thus was accomplished an undertaking, which secured a free passage for troops and war-material over that broad and dangerous river.

As soon as the investment of the citadel had been decided upon, I received orders to prepare a battering-train of fifty pieces of ordnance for the operation—a duty of much labour and difficulty, in consequence of the local disadvantages attending it. The heavy guns and materiel were first to be disembarked from transports lying in the harbour of Passages, and transhipped into *chasse-marées* for conveyance along the coast to the Adour. From these vessels, the guns and ordnance stores were then to be disembarked, to await removal when the batteries were completed.

I received at Passages all the assistance that was in the power of Admiral Penrose to afford; but the naval force was so scantily organized, that it was inadequate even to the service for which it was stationed there; and it was only by employing night and day the exertions of working parties from the transports, a corps of Civil Artificers, and three companies of Artillery, that this onerous operation could be completed, so as to cause as little delay as possible in the contemplated operations against the fortress.

The batteries were completed under the direction of Colonel Elphinstone of the Engineers and the park of artillery, with ample supplies of ammunition, was under the command of Colonel Hartmann of the German artillery. From the undulating nature of the ground between the river and the citadel, we had deemed it impossible for the enemy to discern the site we had chosen for the magazine, which was as near as possible to the batteries, and covered by the slope of a hill.

It had been often observed that an iron cage was suspended from the flag-staff of the citadel, but beyond remarking the circumstance, no importance had been given to it, until the explosion of two shells close to the magazine drew attention to the direction from whence they were thrown. Then for the first time it was discovered that the iron cage contained a man, whose telescope commanded the whole of our position. "Jack in the box" as the soldiers called him, now became a personage of much importance, inasmuch as the hoisting up of his iron frame-work was the signal for dropping shells into the midst of our working parties. The compliment was returned on our side; and a six-pounder having been brought to the precise altitude of "Jack in the box," a few well directed shots took effect upon his hard skin, to the annihilation of his peeping propensities.

The investment of the citadel had not been effected without some hard fighting, which fell on the Germans under General Hinuber. They took possession of the Church of St. Etienne, and some houses that had been fortified by the French, who opposed a gallant resistance under the Governor, Count Thouvenot. The guards were equally successful in driving the enemy from the fortified posts he occupied in front of the fortress; and, from this period, the 29th of February, until the 6th of April, when the heavy guns were ready for removal from the park to the batteries, nothing beyond the firing kept up upon our working parties, and a few unimportant sallies from the garrison took place.

Whilst Sir John Hope was thus occupied in front of Bayonne, Lord Wellington, with the main body of the army, was moving on towards the southern capital of France. It may be said that Soult was the only obstacle to impede his progress; for the inhabitants soon appreciated the admirable regulations that insured safety to property, and respect to person, and were, if not friendly to the invading force, at least, passive.

On the 27th of February, the French Marshal made a stand at Orthes, where he was attacked by Wellington and completely defeated. The battle was bravely fought, with severe loss on both sides; and for the first time during the war, Wellington received a wound from a spent ball. While Soult, with his beaten army, retreated upon Aire and Agens, Beresford, accompanied by the Duke d'Angoulême, who had arrived at head-quarters, was sent with two divisions of the army to occupy Bordeaux. That royalist city greeted with enthusiasm the presence of a Bourbon Prince, and the *drapeau blanc* replaced the tricolore on the spires and towers of the ancient buildings.

From Agens, Soult had been forced by the allies upon Tarbes; but towards the middle of the month of March he was so closely pressed by Wellington, who had received strong reinforcements from the Spaniards, that the French Marshal, after an unsuccessful combat, marched upon Toulouse, destroying the bridges on his route. This circumstance retarded the pursuit of the allied army, and afforded the enemy time to fortify a position in front of that city. It was not until the 28th, that Wellington arrived before Toulouse, and taking up a position on the left bank of the Garonne, the hostile armies stood, the one preparing for attack, the other for defence.

CHAPTER XXII

A DAMAGING SORTIE

THE great commercial city of Bordeaux was now occupied by a division of the allied army, under a British General. In sight of the southern capital of the Empire, waved the united national colours of England, Spain, and Portugal, under a British chief, whilst a formidable mass of war materiel was ready to force open the strong frontier gates of Bayonne's frowning citadel, which contained twelve thousand veteran defenders. A momentous era in the proud history of our arms had dawned, and England's sun of glory shone upon the defeat and humiliation of her foes. At this crisis, when a brief space would probably have sufficed to bring to a focus the brilliant combinations of a Wellington's genius, "a change came o'er the spirit of the dream."

Napoleon abdicated, and peace was restored to the war-sick world.

There are few things that are capable of pressing a stonger conviction of the pigmy confines to which the mind of man is limited, than the reflection that those men of war, Wellington and Soult—agents in the hands of destiny, whose only aim had been to plot, contrive, and execute means of annihilation to each other, with all the strength and energy of devoted hatred, over a series of years past, were powerless as infants to develop the events of three days before them. Had this limited prescience been granted to them, both France and England would have been spared the deplorable loss of their brave sons at Bayonne and Toulouse.

Upon this melancholy page in the History of the War, opinions will ever remain divided as to whether or not the knowledge of the events that were passing in Paris had reached the French and British Commanders. It is an indisputable point that the armistice had not been officially communicated to the hostile parties; but it is difficult to believe that either could have been ignorant that Napoleon's power was crumbled into dust, and that every day— nay, every hour, might bring confirmation of the rumour, already widely spread, of the suspension of arms.

Be this as it may, on the 10th of April, the battle of Toulouse was fought. Soult was forced from the strong position he occupied, and retired with his army into the city, which on the following night he abandoned. On the 12th, despatches arrived announcing to both armies the restoration of the Bourbons; an announcement, which, had it reached but two days earlier, would have saved eight thousand gallant soldiers, who fell a sacrifice, either to the fatal procrastination of a messenger, or to the too anxious anticipation of conquest. Nor did the useless effusion of blood end here: Sir John Hope, in consequence of the rumours that had reached him at Bayonne, delayed to arm the batteries for the attack on the citadel. Late on the 13th, he received intelligence of the armistice; but omitted on that evening to communicate it officially to Count Thouvenot, the Governor, under the conviction that he was also cognizant of its existence.

It is a most improbable circumstance that this French officer should have remained in ignorance of an event, news of which had been dispatched from Paris as early as the 7th instant, and must have been heard of by the many emissaries he employed without the citadel; for, although the fortress was invested, there was no possibility of preventing individuals from holding communication with those outside.

It is, moreover, a strongly suspicious circumstance, that during the six weeks of investment, no sortie from the citadel should have been made, until the fatal night of the 13th, when three thousand of the garrison rushed from their stronghold with no defined object in view of ultimate advantage, beyond glutting their pent-up feelings of vengeance upon the besiegers.

The roar of artillery from the citadel, and the clang of musketry summoned Sir John Hope, in the dead of night, from his bed to his saddle bow; and accompanied by the officers of his staff—amongst them the present Adjutant-General, Sir John Macdonald—he spurred onwards in the direction of the firing, for there was no other guide than sound to lead to the point of attack. While thus advancing through a narrow road, with high embankments on either side, a moving mass was heard approaching in the opposite direction. "They are the Portuguese," observed the General. As he spoke a volley was fired, and he was wounded; his horse dropping down dead at the same moment, entangled him in his fall, and as, in the suddenness of the *mêlée*, his staff had scrambled up, as best they could, the sides of the road, the General was taken possession of by the enemy.

A detachment of the guards now came rapidly up from the rear, and were firing upon the foe, when Hartmann, of the German artillery, who had himself just been wounded, called out at the top of his voice: "Don't fire, by Gott! you will kill the General." The injunction was not in time to prevent the gallant Hope from receiving a second wound from our own men in the vain attempt to rescue him. He was carried off a prisoner into Bayonne.

Among the mournful results of this wanton expenditure of human blood was the loss of the veteran General Hay; this beloved and esteemed commander had braved, and escaped the dangers of many a hard fought day in the Peninsula, and fell a victim, when the din of war was exchanged for a triumphant peace, to the savage *fanfaronnade* of a conquered foe. On that night the gallant General visited the pickets, infusing into the hearts of his old comrades in arms the happiness with which his own was inspired. "No more fighting, my lads," he exclaimed; "now for our homes, wives and sweethearts." His own family had just arrived from Lisbon, and were within a mile of the spot where he stood.

Midnight came. The stillness of that hour was broken by the musketry of the advanced posts. The General hastened with his aide-de-camp to the point from whence it proceeded, and concentrated his small force in the church yard of St. Etienne;

the enemy had issued from the citadel, and were pouring down in numbers.

"Steady, my boys, steady," shouted the veteran Commander; "we shall soon be supported." His voice was heard no more, and a soldier, stooping in the direction where he had stood, found the corpse of his General stretched across a grave. Dearly was his death avenged; and after a carnage of several hours, the French were driven back to the very walls of the citadel at the point of British bayonets.

The morning of the 14th dawned in beauty on a ghastly scene. As nature, purified and refreshened, follows in the track of the death-winged simoom of the desert, so seemed to burst forth the sweet serenity of a spring morning, to oppose its contrast to the ravages of the past night. Under the calm blue sky lay the stiffened corpses, and still writhing victims of the strife of man. A few hours afterwards the tidings of peace were re-echoed from thousands of tongues, and the slaughter of so many brave men in this last scene of a protracted war, left—except in sorrowing hearts—no trace on our memory beyond a passing cloud.

CHAPTER XXIII

JOURNEY TO TOULOUSE

AS soon as peace was proclaimed, active preparations commenced for the removal of the battering-train and materiel that had been collected with so much difficulty and labour before the walls of Bayonne, and as soon as all the arrangements were completed, I received orders to join the head-quarters of the army at Toulouse. After resigning my responsibilities as Military Commissary into the hands of Colonel Hartmann, I bade adieu to the gloomy fortress that reared its head, like a huge funeral monument to the memory of the slain, and accompanied by a young officer of my department, we pursued our journey on horseback to Toulouse.

The first night, we halted at Dax, an insignificant and dirty town, where we were destined to receive incontrovertible evidence that the first impressions of English childhood,—uniting frogs and Frenchmen in an indissoluble union—are not wholly founded upon national prejudice; inasmuch as a very *appétissant* dish of these little amphibious gentlemen took a distinguished position on the supper table at the *auberge* where we alighted. A certain degree of clairvoyance enabled me to fathom the mysteries of the tempting plate; but my companion asserted that it was a *fricassée de poulet*, and treated it accordingly, with all the vigour of a keen appetite. When at length appealing to the *chef de cuisine* he was placed in possession of the fatal certainty, no wrath could equal his, and it was only with difficulty that the unreasonable propensity he had—in common with most Englishmen—of chastising others because they differed from himself in taste, could be kept in proper subjection. However, even wrath gave way to the native weakness of an English stomach, worked upon by a firmly-fixed antipathy, and the poor fellow's inside was consequently reduced to a vacuum, that rendered it most unjust that a charge for supper should have been included in his bill.

From that moment "grenouille," was a word of aversion and loathing, that baffled all argument or remonstrance to overcome. Like the gentleman who fancied himself a tea-pot, or the monomaniac of more recent date, who believed himself pursued by inveterate enemies, so did my companion hear in every sound a croak, and see in every dish a delicate hind leg.

The roads in the south of France are as if designed as a wholesome restraint upon the impatient curiosity of travellers. A straight unbroken line, with trees and broad ditches on either side, forms the boundary of sight both before and behind; and when hope whispers that beyond the boundary, a turn in the road must open some changing prospect to the wearied eye, behold another line, equally straight, and apparently as interminable as the last, appears as if in mockery.

During this locomotive penance, the discordant rejoicings of millions of frogs greet the traveller on every side. In vain he seeks by spurring his horse, or urging on the postillion, escape from the sounds that assail him from the rear. Each step in advance adds to the strength of the chorus, and thus he journeys on, with senses so bewildered, that he can scarcely make out whether he is indeed flitting through a country, that has been designated *la belle France*, or through some strange place beyond the precincts of this globe, to which tormented spirits are consigned. It may be supposed that under these circumstances, my companion, during our second day's ride—the early part of it through a flat and marshy country—received no impression likely to reconcile him to his repast of the previous night, and I confess, that without having the same unpleasant recollections, I could find nothing to say in favour of *la famille grenouille*.

We had intended to reach Tarbes on the second night, but a lovely bit of Pyrenean scenery, peeping at a distance, like a pretty face intruding on one's solitude, was, as the last might be, irresistible, and we left the straight ugly road with its ditches and their noisy inhabitants, to plunge into a charming valley, rich in every production of the sweet south, and affording a shade of thick foliage that was most refreshing after a long ride in the mid-day sun.

The majestic barrier of the high Pyrenees, which separates France from Spain, lay stretched in the distance; its outline only faintly perceptible through the hot vapour that clouded the atmosphere. From this giant chain of mountains, others less and less conspicuous came slanting down to meet the rich valley where we stood, forming a scene, in which the sublime and picturesque were beautifully mingled with fertility. In these days, when every traveller is furnished with a guide-book of the country he is exploring, there would be little excuse for taking a wrong road, and insisting, for its beauty's sake alone, that it would lead, in due time, to the right one. But, at that time, the charlatanism of Itineraries had yet to creep from the press, and the way-farer had either to guess his course, or abandon himself to the most alluring, on the principle that, "*tout chemin mène à Rome.*" Acting on the latter theory, we found ourselves still advancing through the valley, as the sun was throwing his glowing rays upon the fair landscape round us. There is nothing like hunger for dragging down the mind from the contemplation of the beautiful to the realities of creature comforts. No one ever heard of a starving philosopher. In this beautiful secluded spot of nature's workmanship, the rudest sign-post that had pointed to Tarbes, and a good dinner, would have carried off the palm even from Goddess of Beauty.

While musing whether to proceed, or to retrace our steps, a party on horseback appeared in sight, consisting of three persons. As they approached nearer, we discovered that the individual who rode a little ahead of the two others, was an elderly female habited in a dress that is still to be seen in the pictures that represent the old French costume before the Revolution of 1789 amalgamated, in one mass of anarchy and disorder, the rigidly defined classes of society in France. A cloth riding dress that buttoned tightly from her throat to the waist, differed but slightly from man's attire. She sat astride on horseback, with whip and boots that heightened her resemblance to the masculine gender, leaving her sex to be guessed at, rather than identified by the straw bonnet and grizzled ringlets that shaded her face.

It may be supposed we did not allow this opportunity to escape of ascertaining to what part of the world our "search of the picturesque," had carried us; and the courteous, but half satirical smile with which the old lady answered our inquiries by "*Messieurs, vous êtes bien loin de Tarbes,*" was very decisive as to our having deviated, not a little, from the right path.

The disappointment that our countenances must have expressed was met with the same winning manner by our new acquaintance, who congratulated herself in terms of politeness— perfectly captivating to our then inexperienced English ears— upon her own *bonne fortune*, in being enabled to carry us off to her husband's château as visitors for the night. Nothing loth, we allowed ourselves to be persuaded by this genuine specimen of *vieille noblesse*; and joining the lady's cavalcade, we pursued our way through a country even more romantic and beautiful than we had previously seen. *Chemin faisant,* our conductress informed us she was returning home with her attendants from a visit to a neighbouring château, when the beauty of the evening induced her to prolong her ride by a *détour* that brought her to the spot where we were ruminating on the chances of passing the night *à la belle étoile*.

Another league brought us in sight of the first French château of any pretensions we had seen, standing on the summit of a wooded hill. The approach was by an avenue of nearly a mile in length, skirted by tall poplar trees, ascending gradually to the iron grating of the court-yard of the château. Two or three old domestics, attired in liveries as ancient as themselves, that had most probably been re-assumed at the first joyful intelligence of the restoration of the Bourbons, were in waiting to open the heavy portals for their mistress.

As we advanced through the extensive court-yard to the grand entrance, I had a specimen of *les anciennes moeurs françaises*,

in which there was so much more of the touching than the
ridiculous—albeit there was a spice of the latter also—that
I never wondered at the profound regret lavished on *le bon
vieux temps*, by some of the most dispassionate and reflecting
Frenchmen.

As the palfrey stopped before the hall-door, an old gentleman,
with the croix de St. Louis suspended from his button hole,
descended the stone steps, and with a *galanterie empressée* that
could not have been surpassed by a devoted lover to his young
affianced bride, bore his elderly partner gently in his arms from
the saddle to the ground, impressing a kiss on each cheek as
she alighted on terra firma. When this conjugal embrace was
concluded, the lady introduced us to her lord, the Comte de S—,
who welcomed us to his roof, by advancing towards us with a
series of low bows; which losing gradually their profundity as the
distance diminished between us, were at length terminated by his
inflicting twin-kisses upon us also; an operation that almost made
me fear he had mistaken the sex of his guests.

Here then, from way-faring travellers on the road side, we
found ourselves welcome visitors in one of the most hospitable
mansions it has been my fate to remember in any land. The
supper was worthy of the high renown of *la cuisine française*;
but notwithstanding the *recherché* appearance of the table, my
companion shuddered as a *fricassée de poulet* made its appearance,
and identifying it with the frogs of previous night, whispered to
me "that is a monster."

The wines of Burgundy and Bordeaux were not only of an age
and vintage that told of their patrician descent, but these valuable
tenants of the cellarage were uncorked with a liberality that almost
partook of profuse extravagance. At last, our host was so delighted
with the homage we paid to the names of Château-Margaux, and
Romani-Conti, that his hospitality seemed to increase beyond the
powers of restraint.

Slipping from the room, he returned with a bottle, so closely
sealed, that it might have been supposed to hold the fatal contents
of Pandora's box. The cork came out loud and full; there was a
moment's expectation, or rather curiosity to see if anything could

be manufactured by art or time better than had been drank on that evening. A small liqueur glass of the precious liquid was handed to our hostess by her attentive spouse. "*Ah! que c'est délicieux,*" said the lady. It was soon our turn to exclaim. "By Jove! it is common rum," said my companion, with more truth than politeness.

"Oui, Messieurs," chuckled the old gentleman, his ear catching the name of the delicate beverage he seemed so much to prize. "*Oui! c'est du rhum, du vieux rhum.*"

"*C'est délicieux,*" repeated the lady. It was some time before the worthy pair could credit the fact of *Messieurs les Anglais* preferring Château-Margaux, and Romani-Conti to rum; and as it afterwards appeared, it was solely from the mistaken notion that all Englishmen were fond of ardent spirits, that these kind people encouraged us in what they thought we liked, even at the expense of their own good taste.

At a late hour, our hospitable hostess conducted us to our sleeping apartments, and it is with astonishment that my eyes turned to the costly furniture, and elegance of taste with which they were fitted up. All previously conceived ideas of French discomforts, and unclean beds dispersed like chaff before the wind, under the gentle pressure of a delicate white satin duvet, the first I had seen; sheets of exquisite texture, and a canopy of celestial blue, that rose to an immense height above my head, supported by flying Cupids.

The superiority of the French in all arrangements that demand the exercise of taste, is now, I believe, generally conceded to them even by the most anti-gallic; but before the opening of the continent to the class of locomotive English, strange notions were entertained of the semi-barbarism of our neighbours; therefore the excess of luxury I was enjoying, in direct contradiction to my pre-conceived prejudices, seemed like the beneficent work of some good little fairy, who held her revels amidst the wild recesses of the Pyrenees.

On the following morning we bade farewell to our kind hosts, and after the exchange of good wishes, and hopes, expressed and felt, of meeting again, we mounted our horses, and, under the guidance of a small country map, that had been brought into second existence from a dusty shelf in the old library, pursued our route in the direction of Pau.

CHAPTER XXIV

AN END TO HOSTILITIES

THE evening was closing in, after a brilliant day of sunshine, when we reached Pau, a city that well deserves its high repute for the advantages of climate it enjoys, as well as beauty of situation. It stands on an eminence, commanding a delightful country that abounds with the necessaries and luxuries of life. The Gave meanders through its fertile plains, and a chain of lofty mountains, capped with snow, rises in the distance, forming a boundary to the attractive picture.

To the sight-seeking stranger, there are few or no objects of interest, always excepting the Castle where the gallant monarch Henri Quatre, made his first début as a fraction of frail mortality, and the tortoise-shell cradle, in which his little Bourbon eyes were wont to close in gentle slumber. The rest of this once royal residence is converted into barracks, and historical recollections are scarcely sufficient to preserve it from the degradation that time and circumstances have inflicted on it.

The beauty of the weather, the extreme comfort of the Hotel de la Poste, and perhaps above these, the enjoyment of liberty after so many years of harness, combined to keep me some days in these seductive quarters; and at that time I could picture to myself no retreat from the cares and activities of the busy world, where man could dream away existence, forgetting and forgot, more happily than at Pau.

The political bias of the inhabitants was as yet undeclared by any public demonstration, and it is possible that their feelings and interests were so contending that it required to be developed by circumstances, even to themselves. On one side weighed the love-fostering traditions of ancestral loyalty, that warm the heart's blood from generation to generation, when cherished in the locality where they first spring. On the other side was to be placed the loss of place and power to many who had identified themselves with the existing order of things; and thus affection for the past, and satisfaction at the present, united to preserve a temporary neutrality.

La salle de spectacle has often been, both in capitals and provincial towns abroad, a chosen spot for the first ebullition of popular feeling; and it so happened that during my stay at Pau, a little dramatic scene of unstudied effect was performed, which struck a chord, that vibrated, like electricity, through a crowded audience. The performance was about to begin, when a French officer in full uniform, and surrounded by several others, called upon the orchestra from the stage-box, to play "Vive Henri Quatre."

A deep silence reigned in the house, the music and the audience remained equally mute for several minutes. No voice *pour ou contre* was raised. At length the long suppressed air burst upon the ear, but in notes so low and gentle, that it seemed as if to plead an apology for its intrusion. A few voices mingled in the strain. The orchestra, emboldened by the few, burst forth with energy, and from that moment apathy was replaced by enthusiasm. From every part of the house, sobs, tears, smiles, and vociferous cheering were seen and heard. White handkerchiefs and ribbons waved from every box. Cries of "Vivent les Bourbons!" rent the air; and in the midst of ecstasy and joy, the restored dynasty was enshrined in the hearts of the citizens of Pau.

The country, as we approached Toulouse, was a perfect garden, rich in cultivation and in produce. The nut-brown faces of the pretty peasant girls were smiling as the blue above them. The corn and vines looked full of promise for the ensuing season; and but for an occasional military convoy that passed us on the road, we should have had nothing to remind us that the clamour and ravages of war had been carried into the very heart of this now peaceful and happy-looking land. Toulouse is a large, well-built, and in many parts a handsome town, and was at that time full of noise and gaiety. The streets and *cafés* were thronged with English and Portuguese officers, and the lounging idleness of the day was generally terminated by balls or *soirées* at night.

Soult's army was cantoned at no great distance, and many of the French officers used to come over in plain clothes, to see what fun was going on, or to pick a quarrel with some unsuspecting Englishman. Now that the roar of cannon no longer broke upon the tranquillity of the plains, some of these gentlemen sought to gratify their dislike to the English by various stratagems; duels were of frequent occurrence, and several gallant men, who had passed unscathed the perils of the war, fell victims to these implacable feelings. In the *cafés*, or at the theatre, which was open every night, might be seen faces worked up for mischief; the curled lip of contempt, or glance of defiance always ready, to direct at some good-humoured group of noisy young Englishmen, who were far from being unwilling to make allowances for the mortified feelings of brave men, and therefore slow to take offence without sufficient cause.

Among many occurrences that took place illustrative of the sentiments of the *vieilles moustaches* towards the new state of affairs, may be mentioned one that placed an English officer in a position of extreme difficulty and perplexity. Major G—, of the horse artillery, having obtained leave of absence to explore the beauties of Touraine, made the selection of a quiet little town for his head-quarters, where some of the French dragoons were stationed. Prudence might have suggested to an English officer, so circumstanced, the propriety of with-drawing from his helmet the emblem of Bourbon restoration—the white cockade; but the precaution was disregarded—not from a wish to humiliate others—for no such unworthy motive could have found an entrance in the honourable mind of Major G—, but from an intention to adhere strictly to the orders of Lord Wellington upon the subject.

Many were the fierce looks darted upon *la cocarde blanche* by the soldiers, as they passed this obnoxious tell-tale of many a battle lost; but it was left to a still fiercer defender of the *tricolore* to bring to an issue the right of a British officer to sport the detested token of legitimacy in a town where some few staunch hearts still beat for the colours under which they had bled.

It was in one of the streets of this small town that Major G— was arrested in his walk by three French officers, who, with mock courtesy, inquired if he admired the new country in which he found himself. The reply was made with the mildness that characterizes an English gentleman; but this did not suit the purpose of the Frenchmen. "You are, perhaps, come to teach us our duty to our monarch," said one of the party, pointing in derision to the white ribbon in Major G—'s helmet. The latter replied, with calmness, that military man he had no alternative but to obey his General's commands.

"Your General has no power here," vociferated the speaker; and suiting the action to the word, he raised his arm and tore the cockade from its place.

The sensitive feelings of a British officer at this gross outrage may be more easily conceived than described. To chastise the offender on the spot was not in his power, for his side arms had been left at the *auberge*; and no friend was nigh, through whose medium he could seek satisfaction to his offended honour. While thus perplexed, and smarting under the sense of injury, his first idea was to bring his servant, a soldier in his troop, as *témoin* to the affair that he felt was inevitable; but second thoughts are in most cases preferable to the first impulses of excited feeling; and calm reflection pointed out to Major G— a course more in unison with his rank as an officer, and more congenial to his mind as a gentleman.

Acting on these second and better thoughts, he wrote to the Commandant, related the outrage he had received, and called on him as a soldier and a man of honour, to be his friend in bringing him face to face with the individual, who had so grievously insulted him. Between brave and right thinking men, there is a free-masonry, without its mysteries; and the Commandant of this small town in France felt the regret of a brave man, that to a brave man an affront should have been offered.

He wrote in reply that he should have been happy to have been the friend of an English officer under circumstances of so

peculiar a character; but added, that such an extreme measure was
no longer necessary; the offender had been placed under arrest
by himself as soon as the circumstance was reported to him; and
that he had already dispatched a courier to Paris for instructions
how to dispose of him. Thus ended an affair that was calculated
to have produced fatal results, but for the intervention of the
French Commandant, whose discernment marked the difference
between a calm and dignified bravery, and the blustering of an
over-officious zeal.

It was during the occupation of Toulouse the British troops, that
the design was formed of sending a considerable force to America,
and orders were issued to prepare a military equipment for the army
that was to embark for that destination under Sir Rowland Hill.
This equipment devolved on myself to re-create out of the military
stores that had been employed in the Peninsula. It was at Bordeaux
that I commenced and completed this extensive preparation for
the expedition that I had orders to accompany. The convoy was
on the point of sailing, my baggage was even embarked, when it
was decided that the scale of magnitude on which the expedition
was mounted, should be decreased. I consequently consigned my
duties to a junior officer, and returned to the head-quarters of the
army which was on the eve of dispersion.

CHAPTER XXV

BACK IN ENGLAND

THE moment was now arrived when the confederate armies were to break up their cantonments in France. The Portuguese and Spaniards returned to their own countries. The Commander-in-Chief took leave of his brave troops at Toulouse, to assist at the deliberations that were being held in Paris, and all the army was in movement towards home. The infantry embarked for England at the nearest ports. The cavalry and brigades of artillery traversed France by easy and pleasant marches to attain the short sea-voyage between Calais and Dover, while some of the young staff officers, with both time and money at disposal, sought the pleasures and novelties of Paris previously to their return.

It was a moment of strange excitement, this sudden transition from war to peace, from daily intercourse of men, one with another, to a separation that might be for ever. Then, appeared too, for the first time, those pantings for distinction, and petty heart-burnings that invariably follow in the train of despatches and gazettes. Many were nobly worthy of the honours they obtained; and others, who were equally deserving, were passed over for those who were not so; for, in our army, such was the nature of systematic regulations, that no man could receive a mark of distinction—however brilliant the action he might have performed—unless he came within the pale of rules framed in cold blood by government secretaries at home; for instance, an officer who had been in any kind of command at five battles, even had he peeped at them through a hedge, or showed his back instead of his front, was entitled, by right, to a distinguished badge of knighthood,[1] while the most daring achievements could meet with no reward at all, because never having been of course specifically anticipated, neither could they be specifically provided for by official decree.

If the gallant Macguire had survived his chivalric leading of the forlorn hope against the walls of St. Sebastian, would any mark of distinction have been coupled with the admiration his conduct excited? The best answer will be that Colonel Jones, the young engineer, who with conspicuous gallantry led the way at the same siege, for others to follow, and who there found himself alone a prisoner on the hostile walls, who served throughout the war, a distinguished member of his gallant corps, remains, at this distant period, without one outward sign of the honour he so justly gained on that memorable occasion; but, worse than this, was the neglect of reward to the British soldier; he, the brave, the faithful, the enduring, even with the disadvantage of the cold and blighting shade under which he fights.

No hope of promotion stimulates his heart to action. No badge of honour in perspective, nerves his arm to deeds of valour;[2] he shows bravery because it is the inherent quality of his nature—a quality that he is no more capable of divesting himself of, than he is capable of laying down his life and resuming it at will—a quality that might almost be denominated brute courage, but for the short step that divides it from heroism; and yet, to ascend that short step man's moral feeling must undergo as complete a change as that which metamorphoses brute courage into heroism. To effect this change was the study of Napoleon Bonaparte; to crush it was our military policy. Bonaparte, who owed his greatness to the power he possessed of reading the hearts of men, and rendering them subservient to his purposes, well knew that ambition is the spur to action, and therefore did not hesitate to place before the longing eyes of the drummer-boy, the glittering *croix d'honneur*, that only awaited to be won before it hung suspended to his plebeian breast. The enthusiasm thus inspired amounted almost to mental delirium, and many of the French soldiers, who, in our ranks, would have differed in no degree from the common clod-poles of the earth, were led to perform almost supernatural acts of individual heroism, under the enchanted influence of the *croix d'honneur*; whereas the British soldier, instead of wearing on his return from the wars in the Peninsula, the cross that would have linked his humble name with that of Wellington, brought back to his native land a thread-bare jacket, an empty purse, and a toil-worn countenance. These were the only honours that distinguished the soldier of the Peninsular war.

It was in July that I again set foot on the shores of England. London was at that time the head-quarters of the Peninsular officers, lingering for a few days in the crowded hotels, previously to a final dispersion to their respective homes. During this brief space, many were the farewell dinners that took place between friends who had shared the dangers of the war; but at these meetings, the gay hilarity of a campaigning party was wanting. Many had to mourn the breaking up of their boyhood's home, and the annihilation of the bright prospects that hope had promised on returning to it; while to others, time had touched with a rude hand affections that in the distance still wore the freshness that graced them at the parting hour. It is such shocks as these that revolutionize the heart of man; the bright dream of young life, which may be called the poetry of youth, then dies away, and a stern, harsh view of life's realities succeeds it.

It was at one of these military reunions that I fell in with Lieutenant P—, a young officer, belonging to my friend Græme's regiment, the 89th, which had just returned from America. From him I learnt that the noble-hearted Græme was no more; he fell on the field of honour, leaving a name that will ever remain engraven on the hearts of those who loved him. The circumstances attending his death were such as to lead the mind to contemplate, with greater reverence than we are inclined to feel on such subjects, the mystical link that unites our spirit here to its eternal abode. I wrote down, at the time, the details of what was to me so deeply melancholy an event, in the words of our mutual friend P—, who narrated it as follows:

"We were in America under the orders of General Drummond, and the flank companies of the 1st and 89th regiments were sent up the interior of the country to dislodge the enemy from a position he had taken up, and strongly fortified. We commenced our march on a severe morning in the depth of winter, and I remarked that Græme was silent and out of spirits. His heart was usually so joyous, his spirits were so exuberant with life and happiness, that I bantered him on the fit of sentimentality he had assumed, but to no purpose. He could not be cheerful, and twisting out of his cap a little bugle that ornamented it, he said to me with a sad smile: 'Here, P—, keep this for my sake.' I did take it, and I know not why, but his sadness extended itself to me. I saw he had a presentiment he should fall, and in a strange, unaccountable manner, I shared his feelings.

"From the severity of the weather, and the ground being covered with snow, our march was fatiguing in the extreme, and Græme, who commanded the light company of his regiment, had occasion to reprimand several of the men for disorderly and insubordinate behaviour, which would probably have increased to mutiny, but for the love they bore him. To one fellow, who was more unruly than the rest, Græme sharply applied the epithet of 'coward,' alluding to a prior affair, in which some reports had been made upon this man's want of energy. The soldier looked sulkily at him, but made no remark. When we came up with the enemy's works, a murderous fire was opened on us, as we traversed the deep ravine that separated us from the heights he occupied. Every one of our officers, with the exception of Græme and myself, had been picked off by the concealed rifles of our opponents, and we alone remained to lead on to the attack. For a moment we placed ourselves under the slope of a hill, to prepare for a desperate effort to carry the position; retreat or surrender being alike impossible. My gallant friend was rallying his men to the charge, when the poor fellow who had patiently borne the opprobrious name of 'coward,' dragged himself to the spot where Græme stood, staining, as he moved along, the whiteness of the snow with the blood that poured from his wounds. Standing erect before his officer, he said: 'Sir, am I now a coward?' and dropped down dead at his feet.

"Never shall I forget the expression of self-reproach and sorrow that poor Græme's face wore, as for a moment he contemplated the fallen soldier who lay stretched before him. Then, suddenly springing forward, he exclaimed, 'Now, my lads, follow me!' The next moment, 'Oh God!' escaped from his lips, and he fell to the earth. A ball had struck him in the shoulder, traversed his body, and found its way out just below the hip. I rubbed his lips and temples with snow, and used every means to restore animation; but his noble spirit had fled. The rest of us, reduced to eight in number, were made prisoners by the enemy; but we were allowed to carry with us the remains of our gallant comrade; and when we stretched his lifeless corpse at a little distance from the bivouacking party, one of their officers, a rough, hard-featured man, wept, as I well remember, in contemplating the noble countenance and placid smile of that ever-to-be lamented friend. We dug for him a soldier's grave in the vast wilderness, and watered it with our tears. No monumental marble marks the spot; but as long as memory lasts, his name will there be inscribed and cherished."

1. The absurdity and injustice of this regulation was most conspicuously shown in the Royal Engineers. This distinguished corps lost, during the war, from the peculiar exposure attendant on its duties, a greater number of officers than composed its original force. No officer in command survived five battles. Consequently, although some were fortunate enough to survive four, they were debarred, by the regulations, from participating in the honours that were not only due to their meritorious services, but conferred upon many others less deserving.

2. These observations refer exclusively to the soldiers of the Peninsular war; for it appears that in later days it has been deemed expedient to strike medals in commemoration of actions, that in those days would scarcely have found their way into the Gazette. Whether modem liberality proceeds from compunction for the past, or from the rising generation requiring more active stimulants than their fathers did, is difficult to say; one thing is certain, that the veterans of the Peninsular army, who shared the dangers of their great commander on the battlefield, who encircled his brow with laurels, who gained for him, by their invincible bravery, an imperishable renown, who upheld with him the honour of their country's name, those veteran soldiers had a just and undeniable claim on their great commander, and should have obtained, through his recommendation, some special distinction that England would gladly

and proudly have bestowed, at the bidding of one on whom she had lavished so many substantial proofs of her gratitude. Too many years have elapsed to render such distinctions now, conducive either to the honour of the great commander, or to the veterans who served under him. Attempts have been made, and recently, to wrench from a reluctant hand the payment of a debt which, like many others, has been annulled only by the defrauding statute of limitation; and when memory recalls the many gallant soldiers who now lie mouldering in the dust, and who, by sharing in the claims, shared also in the disappointment of their non-requital, there remains but little sympathy for the remnant that would at this late period seek justice, after thirty years' patient submission to her absence.

CHAPTER XXVI

THE COVE OF CORK

THE stirring scenes of the Peninsula had not long been exchanged for the ease and idleness of a home-life, when I received orders to join the forces in America, under Sir Edward Pakenham; and having most vexatiously lost my passage in the Statira frigate which sailed from Portsmouth unexpectedly, with Sir Edward Pakenham and Sir Alexander Dickson on board, only a few hours before my arrival there, the Port-Admiral recommended me to proceed in the Swiftsure, seventy-four gun ship, under sailing orders for Barbadoes with a convoy; he, at the same time, promising to send out directions to insure a passage from thence to the Gulf of Mexico. By pursuing this course, the Admiral thought it probable that I should arrive at my destination almost as soon as the Statira; but hopes and promises at sea are amenable to the winds and waves; and at the expiration of one month, after encountering in the channel very severe gales, the Swiftsure and her convoy were again anchored at the mother-bank.

At this time, fresh orders reached me from the Ordnance, with instructions to disembark, and proceed to Cork, where a force of seven thousand men were assembled, under orders for America; together with a convoy of transports laden with artillery and military stores, of which I was directed to take charge, for the same destination. For this purpose I embarked in a packet from Bristol; and after three days' pitching and tossing, we entered the Cove of Cork. Here I caught my first glance of "The Emerald Isle;"

"The first gem of the sea," upon whose soil, wit and impudence luxuriate as indigenous plants, in the rich manure of Ignorance and Sloth.

Notwithstanding that the month of December had robbed of their green clothing, the hills that stretch to the very margin of the water, the magnificent spectacle of this fine harbour was increased by the number of men of war and transports that plunged and heaved upon its ruffled waves. Two bold headlands, strongly fortified, guard its entrance; and a number of small islands, used for military depôts, rise from the surface of the waters, giving variety and interest to the scene.

The town of Cove faces the entrance to the harbour; it is sheltered by a steep hill, up the side of which it climbs, in irregular zig-zags, and was remarkable, at that time, for little but its poverty and the bustle and activity that prevail in all spots contiguous to a harbour, where Jack-tars are lying at anchor within sight.

As the packet passed Cove, which was the nearest spot to the scene of my duties, I jumped into a boat that pushed off to me from shore, and certainly thought that the whole begging population of the country had turned out to welcome me to "Ould Ireland;" moreover, that they had assumed for the occasion a masquerade variety of poverty-parading costumes.

A red handkerchief tied under the chin was, I observed, a favourite head-dress with most of the elderlies of both sexes; and to many, a sheet, a blanket, and, in some cases, coarse serge swathed round the body, performed the office of cloak in its literal meaning, of concealing what it was thrown over.

Age, ugliness, disease, and idleness, each performed its respective part, with the originality of design and earnestness of execution that I was prepared to meet in the Irish people; for in truth, I was primed with the expectation of having my ears greeted with a continuous volley of *bons mots*, talented *bullisms*, and witty repartees, discharged at the expense of the stranger's pocket, and sometimes of his *amour-propre*.

"Och! sure yer honour is come among us to lave yer good heart in the shape of a tin-penny."

"An honourable young gintleman most intirely ye are, Achrone!"

"Help a poor widdy woman with her siven fatherless childre for the love of the sweet beautiful mother that bore ye."

"Darlint, ye'll lave the light heart in my bussom, and good luck to ye."

"Dacency—dacency, don't bar up intirely his honour's way. Is it to the hootel yer honour would wish to be beguiled; faith, it is a swate illigant place for the quality, and kept by a jewel of a woman, who'll deem it an honour to be a convanience to a jintleman, quite intirely."

"Och! manners, Jim, none of yer gambolling, to fling an impedence in the face of a lone widdy, ould as she may be. Mother Broadway, good luck to her, is convanient to all gintlemen that belong to the ra'al quality and know who's who."

Amidst a little suppressed mirth, at this Hibernian introduction to the merits of Mrs. Broadway, and many groans, I made my way through the throng at the sacrifice of a few tinpennies, and entered the little inn where mother Broadway, as she was familiarly called, presided as hostess.

"And sure yer honour is welcome, barring the dirt on yer boots," were the first words uttered as I introduced myself to a clean, buxom, elderly woman, of about sixty years of age, whose countenance offered, in the still bright complexion, grey eye, and vivacious expression, a good specimen of Irish comeliness.

"What will it plaze yer honour to axe for to ate?" was the question of a very pretty roguish-eyed little waiting maid, rejoicing in the name of "Molly."

"Anything you have got to give," was my answer.

"Why sure, anything manes nothing," said the girl, uttering a truism that nature, and not the world, had taught her—"sure the house is full of dainties, if yer honour would take the throuble jist to move yer tongue to call them."

"Have you a mutton-chop?"

"Och faith, and its thrue that the last was aten this morning by a dandified chap intirely, from the great ship yonder—a mighty dilicate appetite that could ate nothing but mate."

"Well then, give me a chicken."

"A chicken, yer honour! Faith, the only chicken we've got is the old cock, that joys his liberty in the yard; and hard's the bit he'd make for the like of yer quality."

"I have no objection to some fish, if you have neither flesh nor fowl."

"Ochrone!" whined out Molly, in a tone of deep despair, while her eyes glanced fun all the time: "Ochrone! that ill-luck should have crept into the house jist as yer honour first made acquaintance with it. Ne'er a fish would let himself be catched this blessed week past; and Denis O'Sullivan says, they are kaping theirselves, like good Catholics, to be aten in Lent."

The debate between Molly and myself, on the subject of possibles and impossibles, appeared further than ever from conclusion; nor was I sorry when mother Broadway stepped into the council, and congratulated herself that "although her house had been unhandsomely divesticated, she allowed, of flesh, fish, and fowl, by the unmannerly spalpeens from the ships—bad luck to them—she had "a duck" she could recommend for his honour's supper."

My first introduction to Erin, at mother Broadway's Hotel at Cove, was certainly ill-calculated to impress me with an exalted view of the "iligances" of Irish life; but what a rich compensation for torn window curtains, and no bell-ropes, was to be found in Molly's native blarney, from which I received my first, my virgin impression, of Hibernian humour.

"Pray, Molly, can you get my boots cleaned," said I the next morning, after a good night's rest.

"Och, yer honour, sure ye don't mane the thing—your boots claned! Jist now put your pretty face out of the window, and see how dirty the strates are, and then 'twill be—faith—that yer honour will be axing to have yer boots claned!" Molly's logic carried the day.

On sallying forth from mother Broadway's, I was forcibly struck with the animation of the scene before me. No less than eighty men-of-war and transports were lying at anchor, the latter having on board a picked division of infantry, under the command of

General Johnson. Twenty-seven of the transports were laden with field-brigades of artillery, pontoon trains, and every variety of military stores; and these, with a full complement of the field-train department, constituted the charge to which I had been appointed.

The first familiar faces I met were those of my friends Cresswell and Butcher, of the field-train—officers who had gone through the Peninsular war, and were now, like myself, on their way to America. These two gentlemanly and pleasant fellows were on board the "Nile" transport, which I, in consequence, selected for my sea-quarters; and a more united and happy little party never put their sea-stock together, than we formed.

CHAPTER XXVII

DETAINED IN IRELAND

THE fleet was detained by contrary winds in the Cove of Cork for a period of nearly three months, during which time the Blue Peter was flying from the mast-head of the Commodore, as a signal to be under weigh at the first change. So many false alarms had been given during the snatches of absence we made on shore to partake of mother Broadway's currant whisky, and broiled salmon, that frequent escapes made us venturesome, and at length we depended upon the experience of an old weather-wise pilot of the harbour, and the vigilance of our scouts, and bolder grown, ventured to make excursions in the neighbourhood.

Several times we were warned of a movement in the fleet, and returned just in time to weigh anchor and to put to sea; but after tacking about some hours, we were again obliged to return into the harbour, and resume our anchorage as before.

To have quitted Ireland without visiting Cork would have shown an indifference far from being felt to a locality that is identified even more than the capital itself, with Ireland and the Irish; besides, who would forego sailing from Cove to Cork, and thanking nature for the enjoyment she has provided on the charming banks of the Lee?

To vary our excursions we sometimes "jaunted it" to the pretty village of Passage, in a "ra'al Irish sociable," a car so constructed, that two inside passengers are seated back to back, while the driver sits on a seat in front, sufficiently close to amuse his "fare," with a series of questions, answers, and descriptions; at once inquisitive, humorous, and quaint.

Not a castle but has its legend. Not a modern villa but bears the character of its owner in characters as broad and visible as the stones of which it is built, nor a dark glen that does not teem with supernatural inhabitants, through the imaginative and marvel-loving tongue of an Irish car-driver. What he has heard, he improves upon, in the ardour of his recital; and what he is ignorant of, he supplies by an invention of his own, so closely resembling what might be the truth, that it requires an intimate acquaintance with the race to detect the fraud his wit has put upon the stranger.

"What is the name of that high hill, Pat?" said one of my companions to our car-driver, whose tongue had never ceased to enlighten us with information respecting the names, properties, qualities, and private histories of every man, woman, and child we met with on the road. Pat gave a slash to the meagre flanks of the horse he drove, and gained a moment's time by the infliction.

"Was it that hill yonder, yer honour axed the name of? Don't yer honour know the name of the big hill? Och I know it well. It's called the 'ould hill,' because it's been always there."

Another of my excursions was to the far-famed Blarney Stone. Pat acted both in the capacity of driver and guide, and although it appeared very unnecessary for him to increase his share of the gift already bestowed by the talismanic property of the "Blarney Stone," Pat was of a different opinion, and reverentially kissing it, assured me with a comic grin, that "no poor man could have too much! that this world was a big ugly place for the poor, and that three halves of the rich were to be 'blarney tickled.'" After inspecting the old castle, that contains this treasure to the Sons of Erin, we returned to Cork, where McDougall's hotel afforded an excellent sample of Irish comfort and civility.

While the winds were still raging with an apparent determination to detain the fleet within the Cove, news of the most important nature burst upon us most unexpectedly. France had extended her fickle arms to the disturber of the world's peace, and Napoleon Bonaparte was once more at the head of the French nation. For some time after this startling intelligence no change of destination was contemplated for our expedition; but, at the very moment that the weather cleared, the winds abated, and the ocean seemed to smile a welcome, the progress of the fleet was arrested by a telegraphic communication from Dublin, and soon the news spread far and wide, that peace with the United States was concluded, and that England was again about to give her blood and treasure to reinstate a second time upon the throne of France, a race that seemed pursued by an evil destiny.

Orders were immediately issued for the troops to proceed to the Netherlands, and I received directions to disembark on the Island of Haulbowline the whole of the guns, pontoons, and military stores, with the greatest possible speed, to enable the transports to fetch from America troops that had been engaged in that disastrous war. In the space of five days, with the assistance of a strong working party from the flag ship—Admiral Sawyer—and the aid of upwards of a hundred Irish labourers, the transports were cleared, and the wind being favourable, the whole fleet moved out of harbour.

During the progress of this duty I had taken up my quarters at Mrs. Broadway's, and there first learned how easily an Irish heart may be touched by the language of kindness. My intercourse with the native working class was necessarily great. I found them, at first, surly when found fault with, disposed even to be insolent, and their manner of working so deficient in method, that they impeded the progress of each other; but the moment I adopted the system of encouragement, and held out not only the golden prospect of the "poteen," when the day's work was done, but the promise of staying to share in the "farewell cup," then it was that the native character seemed to burst from the weeds that hung about it.

Each man felt his pride less burdensome, because less sorely taxed; and pride being generally the gangrene that gnaws the vitals of the Irish, when once relieved of the calamity, the brighter feelings of their hearts poured forth with freedom. The efforts of these men to deserve praise were immense. I divided them into three parties, numbering them one, two, and three; and, to suit my purpose, offered to bet upon the superiority of the party, whose services I most required at the moment.

The success of my plan exceeded my expectations, and the herculean strength and activity of one fine young fellow was beyond anything I remember to have seen. He took upon his shoulders one of the small guns, a four-pounder; and although bending under the immense weight, spurned the assistance of his comrades, and actually carried it a distance of three hundred yards, from the shore to the depôt. The others would not be outdone; the heavy pontoons were hoisted from the boats, and borne on shore on men's shoulders, with a wildness of energy that it is impossible to describe.

"Who can surpass No. 1?" I called out, at seeing the sinews of the poor fellows' bare legs literally starting from the effects of their exertion.

"The boys of No. 2, plaze yer honour," was roared out by the succeeding party, and then mingling their native humour with their good will, some of them jumped into the pontoons to increase their weight, and were carried on their companion's shoulders into the depôt, where, with reckless, half-savage fun they were thrown, by the bearers, headlong among the stores, to the no small jeopardy of legs and arms.

While the Irish labourer was thus vindicating himself from the aspersion of idleness, which has been unjustly thrown upon him by those who have never seen him under the circumstances of profitable employment, mother Broadway and her little saucy-tongued waiting-maid were equally felicitous in their illustration of the open nature, and generous kindness of the Irish woman. As long as I had my companions with me, and that our boisterous parties, under the immediate inspiration of "currant whisky," partook of the nature of such meetings as generally assembled at the "hostelrie" of mother Broadway, the good dame was imperious, sharp, and often argumentative, on the propriety of allowing "a bait from the Evil One to be thrown in her strame;" but when I was left alone, and engaged in an arduous duty, the kind nature of mother Broadway's heart displayed itself in attentions as numerous as they were refined and varied.

Before the dawn of day, when I would have stolen out to my boat in waiting, without disturbing the inmates, Molly would slyly slip out of the kitchen with a cup of hot coffee, "to keep the cold from my heart, sure;" and always once a day, and sometimes twice, a little boat from mother Broadway's would push off to Haulbowline, the scene of my duties, for the purpose of bringing me some special dainty prepared by her own kind hands.

Having nothing to detain me when my duties at Haulbowline were terminated, I took my passage on board a packet that sailed from Cork, and remembering the discomforts of the last passage, I wrote to mother Broadway—we had already said farewell— begging her as we passed Cove, to send me on board some Fermoy ale, and whatever provender her larder could muster, enclosing at the same time, a five pound note to cover the expenses of my demand.

It was a fine, bright, blowing morning, when the packet started from the quay at Cork; just sufficiently boisterous to hold out a stormy prospect for the next few days; and it was with some little anxiety that I looked for mother Broadway's well-known boat, as we neared the beach of Cove. It was at the side of the packet in the twinkling of an eye; and true to the last, a well-packed hamper was hoisted upon deck.

It was late in the day before I inspected its contents, which consisted of two dozen of Fermoy ale, chickens, a ham, and smoked salmon. On the top lay a little note directed to myself, wherein I found the five-pound note I had sent, and these words:

"Sure! ye wer'nt in airnest to send me the goold, or else ye have no raal notion yet of mother Broadway's thrue Irish heart."

CHAPTER XXVIII

A NEW ALLIANCE

THE excitement caused by Napoleon's escape from Elba had not time to exhaust itself in speculative inquiry as to the measures that Europe would adopt; for, no sooner was the event known to the great powers of the continent, than a gigantic alliance, cemented by England, took place between them—a mighty barrier to the views of the unwelcome intruder!—that required nothing short of his mighty daring, and undiminished self-confidence to resist.

While Russia, Austria, and Prussia, were pressing forward their distant troops to the frontiers of France, England was in a whirlpool of activity, to supply, by a perfect organization of her resources, the deficiency that existed in her numerical strength. The recently terminated war in America had called away many of our veteran Peninsular troops; they had been recalled, but in the interval, the exigency of the moment required that fighting men should be sent over to the continent; and such was the requisition for artillerymen, that at Woolwich there was scarcely a sufficient number left to mount guard.

When, at length, the transports brought back our soldiers from America, they were not even permitted to land, but ordered off to the seat of war, to engage again in those scenes of bloodshed that had been their lot for so many years. Sir Alexander Dickson, of the artillery, had been only a few hours returned to the home where duty to his country had made him almost a stranger, when a messenger arrived from the Master-General of the Ordnance, with orders for him to join the Duke of Wellington's head-quarters in the Netherlands with the least possible delay: the Duke having left directions to that effect.

I was on the point of departure for that country, and, at the request of Sir Alexander Dickson, tarried a day longer to accompany him. We left Woolwich on the 12th of June for Ramsgate, where we found Sir Thomas Picton, superintending the embarkation of his horses on board a small transport that had been placed at his disposal by the government. At that time, it was generally believed among military men that this distinguished officer had reason to be dissatisfied at the manner in which his services had been recognized; and that feelings of wounded susceptibility had weakened the friendship that once united him to the Duke of Wellington.

Nothing can be more false than such an assertion; for although, under such circumstances, Picton would still have been too much the true soldier not to have felt the *prestige* of a Wellington's name, and far too noble-minded to have allowed self to interfere with the interests of the service, yet it would have been impossible for him to have paid the Duke the tribute of affection I am about to allude to, unless he had also loved the man.

The party that met at Ramsgate dined on that day together, and when the health of the Duke of Wellington was proposed, he, who had seen the sparkling eye, and heard the fervent voice of Sir Thomas Picton, as he added an emphatic "and may God bless him!" to the toast, could never have doubted the source from whence the sentiment sprung.

As soon as the tide served, on the same evening, Sir Alexander Dickson and myself embarked for Ostend with this brave man, who was destined to find a hero's grave on the field of Waterloo. As he sat on deck, closely wrapped in his cloak, his eyes were sternly fixed upon the shores that he was fated never to behold again! A melancholy shade overspread his countenance as the white cliffs of Albion faded from his sight; and never has the glorious death of Sir Thomas Picton been spoken of in my presence, without its recalling to my mind how unusually silent and subdued he was, in leaving a country that was soon to mourn his loss.

Early on the 13th we reached Ostend, where a pleasure was in store for me, in the sight of my old friend, Sinclair, of the 44th regiment. This gallant fellow was one of the *élite* of the Peninsular officers; he was in the third division under Picton, and his regiment was one of the foremost columns that advanced to the attack of Badajoz. The captain of the grenadier company having received a severe wound, the command of it devolved upon Sinclair. A sprinkling of daring spirits, such as his, was essential to the success of an enterprise, which, up to that moment, was not only doubtful, but fraught with danger to the military reputation of the great Commander who conducted it.

Sinclair led his men to the very walls of the castle, which poured upon them, from the heights, a murderous fire. Only three scaling ladders were raised against the ramparts, and at that moment of awful suspense which precedes, on such occasions, the ascent to probable destruction, of hearts beating high with life and spirit— my friend sprang to a ladder, followed by the brave soldiers of his company—for soldiers are always ready to share danger to which their commanding officer leads them. On reaching the summit, he found the ladder too short for the height of the parapet; yet, nothing baffled, he crept through an embrasure, and was one of the first who trod upon the walls of Badajoz. Closely followed by his party, a fierce contest ensued between the besiegers and the besieged. Foot to foot the ground was won and lost, and the darkness of night added to the horrors of this scene of carnage.

Although severely wounded, Sinclair still encouraged his men by his voice and example; until overpowered by a second severe wound, he sunk upon the ground, mingled with the dead and dying. In this state, he lay trampled under foot by the combatants, who successively advanced or retreated, as the tide of success ran with or against them. Yet, still as the glare of light flashed from the fire-arms around him, and allowed him to distinguish his gallant followers, still did his voice animate them on, until nature became exhausted, and he sunk into insensibility. It was not until the invincible intrepidity of our troops had surmounted every obstacle, and driven the enemy from his posts, that my friend was discovered at day-light in the place where he had fallen.

This gallant soldier, at a later period, was one of the foremost who escaladed the fortress at the unfortunate attack of Bergen-op-Zoom, and was by the side of the lamented Colonel Carlton, when fighting hand to hand, that officer received his death wound; and yet, Sinclair, whose name is dear to all who knew him as a soldier—whose name is dear to all who know him as a friend, quitted the service of which he was an ornament—a subaltern!

On the evening of the 14th, Sir Thomas Picton, attended by his three aides-de-camp, Captains Tyler, Chamberlain, and Price, Sir Alexander Dickson and myself arrived in Brussels. Who could have imagined, in viewing the gay aspect of that city, that the desolation of war was concealed behind the brilliant scene, or that any thought, save that of pleasure, could intrude on minds apparently so eager to enjoy it? And yet, at the very time, Napoleon's formidable army, under his own experienced generalship, was concentrated on the Sambre ready to advance on the capital of Belgium.

Early on the morning of the 15th the French commenced hostilities by attacking the Prussian outposts at Thuin and Lobez; and after gaining a decisive advantage, advanced upon Charleroi, while the Prussians fell back upon Sombref. The first intelligence of the outbreak of the enemy reached the Duke of Wellington through the Prince of Orange, at about four o'clock on the same day.[1]

The Duke was at dinner when the Prince rode into the court-yard of his hotel in the Rue Royale, and without dismounting from his horse, communicated the intelligence to his Grace, who immediately afterwards issued orders to the several divisions of the army in their respective cantonments, to be in readiness to move at a moment's notice. But no stir or bustle accompanied the important arrangements that were going on. The town was yet in ignorance of the events that had occurred; and such was the tranquil demeanour of the experienced officers, to whom the Duke's orders were given, that hence may be supposed to have arisen the absurd and fabulous report of the Duke of Wellington having been surprised by the enemy, while philandering away his time at a ball given, on the night of the 15th, by the Duchess of Richmond.

Long before the Duke and his staff joined that memorable *fête* every preparation had been made for an immediate movement of the army; and Blucher's despatch, which arrived towards midnight, bearing the intelligence of the enemy's nearer approach, only hurried the conclusion of the arrangements that had been quietly, yet actively progressing for some hours previously.

At that late hour the 5th division, quartered in Brussels, was summoned to arms. This division was under the command of Picton, whose first inspection of the gallant regiments that composed it, may be said to have taken place in the testing presence of the enemy. Even before the sounds of the drum and bugle had called the troops to the rendez-vous, groups of persons were gathered in the streets, to gain some more defined intelligence than the rumours that were beginning to circulate through the town. Nothing positive was known, but everything was feared, and the indistinct hum of voices breaking on the stillness of the night, sounded ominously, like the distant murmur of convulsed elements, that precedes the storm at sea. When, at length, the drums beat to arms, and the troops poured forth from their quarters towards the Place Royale, where they were ordered to assemble, the truth could no longer be concealed, and the night was passed in feverish anticipation of the morrow.

Before the break of day, the rifle corps, headed by the gallant Sir Andrew Barnard, and followed by the brave regiments of Picton's 5th division, and Brunswick's "black horsemen" issued from the gates of Brussels on the road to Quatre Bras, where the left of the Anglo-allied army was menaced by the enemy.

The 1st and 2nd corps of the French army were under the command of Marshal Ney. This division was intended to attack, in detail, whatever allied troops might present themselves from Brussels, while Napoleon carried the strength of *la grande armée* and the magic influence of his name and presence against the Prussians under Blucher. Had Ney concentrated his troops at Frasnes, which, by using great exertions, he might have done by the morning of the 16th, history would probably have had a very different tale to record of the events of that day. Had the French Marshal even employed the strength he had, of eighteen thousand men, well supported by cavalry and artillery, instead of allowing them to slumber away the night of the 15th on the heights of Frasnes, he might still have carried out the designs of his great master, by attacking the Belgic-Dutch brigade, which formed the extreme left of Wellington's army, and sweeping it from its position before Quatre Bras. The same night his head-quarters would have been at Gemappe. On the 16th, his columns would have been concentrated, and the 1st, 2nd, and 5th divisions of the Anglo-allied army would have been attacked in detail, or forced into a retrograde movement.

On the 17th, Napoleon, who, on that day, forced the Prussians to retire upon Wavre, would have operated upon Wellington's left, and before the concentration of the allies could have been effected, Brussels would have been the head-quarters of Napoleon, and the Belgian army, although at that time no great prize to any monarch, would have ranged itself under the French *tricolore*.

This was the scheme of Napoleon; and that its execution failed, must be ascribed to one of those inexplicabilities in the tide of Fate that no human discernment can solve. As already stated, Ney's disposable force bivouacked on the night of the 15th at Frasnes, and it was only at about one o'clock on the following day, that the French Marshal, uncertain, it is true, of the strength of the enemy before him, shyly advanced some of his light troops in the direction of Quatre Bras, a position that was held by a division of the Dutch, under the command of the Prince of Orange. Not withstanding the superiority of the enemy, this Prince chivalrously maintained his ground until the arrival of Picton's division; and it ought to be one of Belgium's proudest recollections that her hereditary Prince, so young in years, yet old in the experience of a soldier, should have struck the first blow against the violators of her liberty.

The appearance on the field, of the British regiments was the signal for the opening of a tremendous fire from the enemy's batteries. The enemy mustered strong, even from the first, in artillery and cavalry, whereas we were most deficient in both,

having of artillery only two batteries—British and Hanoverian—
of six guns each; and of cavalry—to be depended on in the hour
of need—the "Brunswickers" alone.

This it was that made the battle of Quatre Bras so fatal to the
brave fifth division, which had to sustain the furious charges of the
French Cuirassiers and Lancers, in addition to the sweeping havoc
of artillery from the enemy's heights; yet such was the determined
bravery that was opposed to these unequal odds, that every charge
was repulsed at the point of the bayonet, and every murderous
gap filled with the same steady coolness that might have been
displayed on a field-day.

As if it had been the caprice of Fate to test to the utmost the
endurance of the 'superb division,' the already preponderating
force of Ney's cavalry was increased by the arrival of two thousand
of Kellerman's heavy cavalry division, while no reinforcement of
the British troops came to cheer the hearts of the devoted men,
who were nobly upholding their old Peninsular fame.

Nothing henceforth could have sustained this fearful conflict,
but the unconquerable spirit of the lesser number. That spirit,
unflinching, unshaken, never for a moment flagged during the
unequal contest. It animated the men to die rather than to yield
an inch of the contested ground; but, as the instruments of
carnage mowed down their ranks, Wellington watched, in anxious
suspense, for the arrival of the more distantly cantoned troops to
reinforce the devoted band.

By six o'clock the first and third divisions, under General Cooke
and Sir C. Alten, and a strong reinforcement of artillery, had
relieved the exhausted fifth division; but the enemy's strength had
been also materially increased by fresh troops, and the fierceness
of the combat raged the more intensely, from the renewed vigour
of the combatants.

Although severely fatigued by a long day's march, the allies
resisted, with indomitable bravery, every effort of the enemy to
force the position of Quatre Bras, and finally, Ney, conscious that
further attempts would prove equally unavailing, withdrew his
troops to the heights of Frasnes, and night threw a veil of darkness
over the field of blood.

1. This information was given to the author about an hour afterwards by Sir Alexander Dickson, who was dining with the Duke of Wellington, when his Grace rose from table to receive the Prince.

CHAPTER XXIX

HARD FIGHTING

THE footing so gallantly maintained at Quatre Bras was effected at a fearful loss to the Anglo-allied force, and at the price of many valuable lives. The Duke of Brunswick nobly fell at the head of his brave "black horsemen," while cheering them on to avenge a father's death and a country's wrongs.

The veteran Colonel Macara, of the 42nd Highlanders, was sacrificed, with two companies of his regiment, to the furious onset of a body of the enemy's Lancers. This charge was with such startling rapidity, that there was not time to include the flank companies, as the regiment formed square to receive it, and direful was the result to these brave fellows. Macara had served in India and throughout the Peninsular War with distinction, and was peculiarly adapted for commanding the hardy clansmen of the 42nd. His stalwart figure and martial countenance were well in character with the mountain-clad warriors he had so often led to victory; and such was the love he bore the regiment that he used to say, he would rather head it to confront the French, than be made the General of a division, in which it played no part. Mortally wounded, the veteran fell amid a host of his own brave soldiers, and right nobly was his death avenged by the survivors of the 42nd, under their next officer in command, the gallant Colonel Dick, who was himself soon afterwards severely wounded.

Some of the regiments of the fifth division were reduced to mere skeletons of their former strength; but gained a glorious compensation in the undying renown their devoted valour won. Maitland's guards and Barnard's riflemen shewed, by the consummate skill with which they took advantage of every change of circumstance, that their practical knowledge of warfare had been acquired in the training school of the Peninsula; while our faithful allies, the Germans, asserted, as they ever have done, by their conspicuous gallantry, their right to participate in the laurels of the British soldier.

While Ney's division was engaged with the allied troops at Quatre Bras, Napoleon was in fierce contest with the Prussians, under Blucher, at Ligny. This battle was one of the most sanguinary of modern times, and waged with unabated fury, from three o'clock till nightfall; both armies bringing to the encounter a hatred that could only be extinguished in death. No quarter was asked or given. The advantage of position was on the side of the French, and although the numerical strength of the two was slightly in favour of the Prussians, yet such was the preponderating influence of the enemy's cavalry, which nearly doubled that of Blucher, and the superiority of his artillery, that it may impartially be affirmed, that in strength, the French army predominated. To render it still more effective, Napoleon sent orders for the first corps of infantry, and Gerard's division of the second corps to march from Frasnes to join *la grande armée*. Of this ill-judged movement, so fatal to the enemy, and so fortunate to the allies, Ney complained, in bitter terms, at a later period, when unjustly reproached for, at best, a cold adherence to his master's cause.[1]

The Prussians fought with an infuriated energy that sprung from the recollection of past humiliation and grievous injury, and the veteran Blucher himself, during the fierce conflict, performed prodigies of personal valour, leading his troops, sword in hand, into the thickest of the fight.

The carnage was terrific on both sides, but greatest on the side of the Prussians, resulting from the disadvantages of ground. At length, unable to withstand the concentrated assault of the whole of the enemy's cavalry, including the veterans of the Imperial Guard, Blucher drew off his army, unmolested by the enemy, who had also suffered severely, and re-forming it at a distance of a mile from the scene of action, retreated under cover of night, and in admirable order, upon Wavre.

The heroes of Quatre Bras bivouacked the night of the 16th upon the ground they had so valiantly made their own; and it was not until the following morning that Wellington, apprised of Blucher's retreat, decided on a retrograde movement, to facilitate the junction of the allied and Prussian armies. This retreat of the troops concentrated at Quatre Bras was effected with so much secrecy, that the greater part of the infantry was beyond molestation, before the enemy was aware of the movement; and it was only when the cavalry of the rear-guard, under Lord Uxbridge, moved off from the ground, that a large body of French cavalry and lancers was sent in pursuit. From that time, a continuous skirmishing was kept up between the hostile cavalry, with little or no results, with the exception of an affair at Gemappe, where the rear-guard, closely pressed by a regiment of lancers, received Lord Uxbridge's orders to charge them. This was done with much spirit, but with ill success, by the 7th Hussars, who, in their turn, received the spirited charge of the lancers, and suffered considerable loss. Major Hodge, commanding the leading squadron, was slain, and the regiment thrown into great confusion.

It was soon manifest that the hussars, notwithstanding the gallantry they displayed, were unequal to the part assigned them. Neither men nor horses were fitted to cope with the novelty of lances and flags; and it was injudicious to order light horsemen to charge the solid wall of bristling lances that was opposed to them. So the result proved. The horses fell back in alarm at the flags that flapped in their eyes; and although several desperate efforts were made to re-form, and the attack was renewed by the hussars, it failed to make any impression on the enemy. Lord Uxbridge then withdrew them from the unequal combat, and ordered the 1st Life-Guards to charge the increasing masses of cavalry that menaced the rear.

Headed by Major Kelly, these gigantic horsemen rushed down the hill upon their opponents, sweeping before them, like an avalanche, every object in their course. Nothing withstood the shock of that magnificent charge. Men and horses, lances and flags, were trampled in the dust together; and driving the enemy to a respectful distance from the retreating columns, the Life

Guards thus secured a free and uninterrupted passage for the allies to the plains of Waterloo.

1. Vide Marshal Ney's letter to the Duc D'Otrante, dated Paris, June 26, 1815.

CHAPTER XXX

HUMAN SUFFERING

IT was growing dark on the evening of the 16th, when a wagon, filled with our wounded men, slowly descended the road that leads from Quatre Bras to Brussels through the Forest of Soignies. The rain was pouring down in torrents from the dark and angry skies; the thunder growled heavily, and the lightning illuminated, at intervals, the gloomy depths of the forest.

It was a fearful storm, and every living creature had sought shelter from its violence, when two females were seen approaching from the direction of Brussels. The youngest was tall, and of a commanding figure, though fatigue and anxiety seemed to have bowed her down, as the lily by the passing blast. Her complexion was white and pure as marble, and the perfect regularity of her Grecian features rivalled the *chef-d'œuvre* of a Canova; but there the resemblance to inanimate nature ceased, and the fevered lip, and anxious eye told of the mockery of art.

No bonnet covered the long dark tresses that fell, matted with the rain, in crazy disorder on her shoulders. A thin white dress was the only protection against the torrents that came rattling to the earth. It seemed as if some horrid vision, some fearful presentiment of evil had beckoned forward this fair being, to meet a fatal certainty. Her companion was of humble class, and her bronzed complexion, and thick cloak of scarlet cloth, spoke of old campaigning habits, acquired under a warmer sun than shone in the skies of Belgium. Mary Gifford looked, and was—the soldier's wife!

In spite of the increasing storm, the two walked on—their silence only broken by the deep-drawn sighs that burst from each, when their attention was arrested by the wagon already mentioned, which approached, slowly jolting over the rough and rutted road.

"My God!" exclaimed the soldier's wife, whose experienced eye could not be deceived as to the purpose of the vehicle before her; "they are bringing off the wounded. Heaven help us, young lady, this is not a sight for the like of ye."

"Oh, mind me not!" murmured faintly her companion; "but ask—ask what news of the 28th regiment." She could say no more, but sank fainting by the road-side.

Mary Gifford, whose feelings, although deeply rooted, were become less excitable, from long acquaintance with the dangers of a soldier's life, advanced to seek the dreaded information.

The irresistible eloquence of grief was not to be mis-understood.

"Whom seek ye, poor woman," said the driver, mechanically stopping his horses as she laid her hand inquiringly on his shoulder. The name—the nearest—dearest, trembled on her lips, but could not escape them.

"I seek," she replied, while her dark complexion assumed a darker hue, as she spoke: "I seek tidings of the 28th regiment."

The driver shook his head.

"Poor fellows, they have been sadly cut up, I hear; but none of them are with me;" and so saying, the wagon jolted onwards in the direction of Brussels.

With anxiety, swelled to agony, the unhappy woman returned to the young lady, who still lay insensible on the bank, where she had placed her. The cold air of approaching night, however, at length revived her to a sense of the mission she had undertaken to accomplish; and with faltering steps, she again endeavoured to advance. Another, and another wagon dragged slowly its sad burthen over the uneven road, and again and again was hailed by the poor wanderers; but night had closed upon this day of trial, and the groans of the suffering wounded as they approached and receded from the spot, stifled the women's feeble efforts to attract attention. Long and dreary was that night; and stretched on the cold damp earth, lay the sinking form of the young and fair Emma C—, who had placed herself under the protection of a soldier's wife, to seek, on the field of the dead and dying, a beloved and only brother.

The morning of the 17th dawned; and with it returned the anxious restlessness of those devoted beings to advance towards the scene of the previous days' combat. Wagon after wagon passed, bearing the mangled victims at the shrine of glory; and into each sad receptacle of mortal suffering, the stern soldier's wife bent a piercing look of inquiry, in which hope and fear were strangely blended. Another appeared in sight—it was open; and the countenances of all within were distinctly visible. A very young man, in the uniform so dear to Mary Gifford, and whose fair hair was dyed in the stream of gore that flowed from a severe sabre wound in his head, raised himself to bend over the side of the wagon as she approached.

"Well, Molly," he said, "we ar'nt quite so cock-a-hoopish just now, as we were yesterday morning."

"And, John?" demanded the woman in the husky voice of deep emotion.

"Hit—badly hit," answered the young soldier. "I saw him on the ground last night very much hurt."

The poor woman groaned aloud, and returned with rapid strides to her young companion. In another hour they were in the midst of the horrors and confusion of the field of Quatre Bras.

Surrounded by the dead and dying, Mary Gifford left her weaker companion to the care of some soldiers' wives, who were assembled round the brandy flagon; and moving forward to a group of men, clad in the well-known uniform, she found herself led, almost unconsciously by a kind supporting arm—for Molly was the favourite of the regiment—to the presence of her wounded husband.

Extended on a litter of straw, and covered with a blanket, lay the gallant Sergeant Gifford; and one look sufficed to tell the distracted wife that all would soon be over with the veteran. A kind smile of welcome flitted over his dying features, at this last proof of devotion from his faithful help-mate.

"Molly," he faintly whispered, as she leant in bitter, but silent grief over him; "this is like you—like what you have ever been to me—the best of human beings. Molly,"—she bent down to listen to his faint voice, "they have shot off both my legs!"

The wretched woman heard no more, but fell senseless on the mutilated form, that one short day before had displayed in a remarkable degree, the strength and health of vigorous manhood.

The wounded man made an effort to raise the devoted wife, who had fallen, without consciousness, on his bosom. A blessing on her head struggled with the parting breath of life, and the British soldier was no more.

When Emma C— was placed under the care of the rough followers of the camp, the excitement of her mind bordered upon frenzy. A flush of crimson overspread her usually pale complexion, and the pensive cast of her large expressive eyes had changed to a feverish and unnatural brilliancy. With vacant stare, she met the inquiring looks of those around her, and gazed, with apparent indifference, on the appalling scene of the previous day's carnage, where the slain were stretched in the stiffened shroud of their own gore. Some she passed unheeded by; others she examined with intense interest.

At length an object arrested her attention; she sprung towards it, clapped her hands, laughed, and throwing herself upon the lifeless form of a young officer, whose uniform was of the gallant 28th, she kissed with frantic fondness the eyes and lips that death had for ever sealed.

"William," she joyously exclaimed, "I have found you at last, and we will part no more. Dearest brother, hearken to that waltz; do you remember that we danced to it at the ball last night?"

Can it be—that the young brother and sister—on whose graceful movements an admiring circle gazed but a few short hours before, as one encircled the other, in all the pure freedom of fraternal love—are here stretched a loathsome spectacle of death and madness?

Short-sighted mortals! look again, and in the picture trace the mercy that Providence has shown to both. To the young soldier who died in the arms of victory, was spared the disappointments, the heart-gnawing evils that as surely attend on after-life as death attends its close.

On the young girl, the loss of an only brother fell gently; for her mind was unconscious of the bereavement, and her disordered fancy created images of past and future happiness. Images that knew no change, and which the cold realities and conventions of the world had no power to destroy.[1]

1. Mary Gifford, one of these heroines of real life, has long since been consigned to the silent tomb, and the fate of Emma C—, may be said to have received its first dark tinge of misfortune on the field of Quatre Bras. For many weeks, her life and reason were despaired of, and when, at length, youth and natural strength gained the ascendancy, and memory once more became the mirror of the past, there was not one drop of sweetness left for her in the cup of life. Her young heart had been bestowed on one whose constancy had drooped before the test of absence and of sorrow, and this last stroke severed her for ever from the joys of the world. In after years, she became a wife, but not of him to whom her faith had been plighted in happier days. And though she performed the task of duty with the sweetness natural to her character, the mournful expression of her countenance, at times, would lead an observer to surmise that her thoughts were then resting on the grave of her earliest affections, the field of Quatre Bras.

CHAPTER XXXI

WATERLOO

HISTORIANS have celebrated, and poets sung, the Field of Waterloo; and as far as it has been possible, have dilated upon the beginning, progress, and result of that eventful battle, until nothing has been left to add to the many glowing pictures they have transmitted to posterity. It is true that all have been subjected, more or less, to the charge of incorrectness, on some particular point or another, and have given rise to contradiction and controversy, nor is it possible that it should be otherwise, when it is considered that information on the details of battles must necessarily be gleaned from individuals, whose individual feelings are interested, and consequently are to be gratified. Leaving therefore such points as admit of dispute to those who have already met on the hostile ground of controversy concerning them, it will perhaps be more interesting to look back upon the plains of Waterloo through that prism only, whose faithful accuracy time has tested; and which brings them to the view of all, as plains hallowed by the life blood of the brave: as plains, on which thousands of deep imbedded recollections linger still.

Vain indeed would be the efforts of the human pen, accurately as it might delineate the leading features of the contest on the plains of Waterloo, to trace even the faintest outline of the feelings that flowed from that vast fount of human suffering. How many have found refuge in the grave from the intensity of sorrow, that mingled with the name of Waterloo. How many have withered in the chill blight of memory, unable to force the sap of life from its strong tenement, and thus dragged on a miserable existence!

Others again—like the sapling that bows to the earth its young head as the raging storm sweeps over it, escaping annihilation by bending to the stroke—were laid prostrate by the sudden wrenching in twain of ardent affection. Sorrowing in deep despair over the field of Waterloo, their grief found at length extinction, in its own violence.

On the morning of the eventful 18th of June, the allies rose from their bivouac on the wet earth—for the night had been a tempestuous one—and prepared to face the formidable enemy that lay stretched, in masses of cavalry and infantry, along the opposite heights. This army, headed by Napoleon, numbered eighty thousand men, and was supported by a well-equipped artillery of two hundred and fifty guns. Moreover, it possessed the immense advantage of being composed of men of one nation; men, bound together by the pride of country, as well as by an enthusiastic feeling towards their sovereign and leader. Whereas, of the allied army under Wellington's command, although but slightly inferior in point of numbers to the French, twenty-five thousand only were British soldiers. The rest were foreign troops; some of which were nobly brave—others were rendered useful auxiliaries by the power of good example; while others again were to be trusted so cautiously, that their absence from the field would only have been felt as a security against treachery.

The hostile armies occupied heights running nearly parallel with each other. The distance that separated them was about twelve hundred yards, and the intermediate ground, or rather valley, formed by a gentle declivity on either side, was richly covered with luxuriant corn.

The allied forces stretched across the high roads that lead to Brussels from Charleroi and Nivelles, having in their rear, at a distance of about two miles, the Forest of Soignies. Their left extended to the hamlet of Ter la Haye, from whence a road leads to St. Lambert by which a communication with the Prussians was maintained. In front of their left centre stood the farm-house and gardens of La Haye Sainte, and towards the centre of their right, the Château of Hougoumont.

The enemy's attack on the latter position at about eleven o'clock A.M., on the 18th, was the commencement of the battle of Waterloo.

At about that hour, a numerous host of tirailleurs advanced close to the wood and orchard of the château, followed by two massive columns of the 2nd corps of the French army, under Jerome Buonaparte. Pressing rapidly through the waving corn, these columns were next seen as rapidly pressing up the slopes that led to Hougoumont; but here they had to deal with British and German valour, and while a detachment of the guards that occupied the house poured upon the assailants a fire calculated to impair the ardour of the assault, the opening thunder of the battle pealed through the air from Cleeves's battery of nine-pounders, stationed on a height, at a distance of about three hundred yards to the left, and a little in advance of the front line.

The leading column was seen to lose its firmness, and to hurry onwards, when a second roar of artillery, from the battery of Captain Sandham, posted on a height that nearly faced the advancing foe, stopped its progress, by laying low the front ranks. Before the rear could fill up the gaps, Cleeves's guns were again at work, and as the two batteries threw, with deadly aim, their showers of spherical and case shot on front and flank, the columns wheeled round, and retired in precipitation and disorder.

Thus commenced the battle of Waterloo; a battle that differed from all others in the sacrifices demanded and conceded during its long continuance, of nine hours. Wellington had taken the best position left to him. It covered the capital of Belgium—it communicated on the left with the Prussians. The undulating nature of the ground was favourable for acting on the defensive until the arrival and co-operation of Blucher, and upon strict adherence to the defensive, the safety of Wellington depended.

Here then was no field for the display of skilful generalship, and tactical knowledge. The one great essential to a Commander so placed, was firmness, and fortunately for the allies, Wellington possessed that attribute in no small degree. The one great essential for soldiers so placed, was blind obedience—which is a habit rather than a principle—and was so rigidly inculcated in the British army by the Duke of Wellington, that he well knew how far he could depend upon its practice in the field.

Necessity demanded that the position of the allies at Waterloo should be maintained, though rivers of blood should flow from its defenders. And more than this; necessity demanded that brave men should stand passively to be slain, nor slay in turn, until, like automatons, their faculties were put into movement by a superior power. This it was, that made the bloody field of Waterloo one, over which angels might have wept. No retaliation was offered by the brave, the young, the haughty, as mutilated and bleeding, their comrades fell in heaps around them. The flashing eye and panting heart, told what the spirit longed to do; but confidence in their leader, and blind obedience to his will, were stronger even than revenge, and like lambs they stood the slaughter, until the word of command roused them to be lions.

During this contest, the French varied their modes of attack, sometimes by advancing columns of infantry, flanked by cavalry, and under cover of a powerful artillery. At such times, our gunners, posted on the rising ground, would throw their missiles, with tremendous effect, among the closely wedged masses, and if driven from their guns to seek shelter in the squares, our heavy cavalry rushed down the slopes, and, with their powerful horses, rode down the mailed squadrons of the foe; while our infantry deploying into line—generally only two deep—would steadily ascend the slope that sheltered it from the enemy's batteries, and facing the advancing mass, until within sometimes only twenty yards, would greet them with a well directed volley. The next moment, the order to "charge" would be responded to by a true British "hurrah," and before the enemy could fly back to his position, the guns, that had been momentarily abandoned, were again at work. Our infantry would then steadily resume its place behind the slopes, often lying down to avoid the fire; and the cavalry having driven back to their own territory the French squadrons, would resume its station, ready to repulse, in the same manner, similar attacks.

At other times, the French cuirassiers advanced in heavy masses, covered by their artillery. As they boldly ascended the slopes, exposed to a murderous fire from the batteries, our gunners were again driven to seek shelter in the squares, or under the limbers of their guns, where many were lanced and sabred.[1] The bold horsemen would then advance, at furious speed, until within a horse's length of our firm and close-knit squares; here they would brandish their long swords in impotent defiance, and often strike the bristling bayonets that stood as barriers to their further advance. Imprecations, screams, and even jests were levelled at the impassable obstruction. Carbines and pistols were discharged in mock revenge; but not a trigger returned the challenge until the word "fire" ran clearly down the line of the menaced square. Then down went the front men and horses of the leading squadron. A well directed fire from the next square threw the rest into confusion, and our cavalry would effectually complete their rout.

Such were the leading features of the day's engagement, in which both armies displayed a desperate valour, that has never been surpassed. The position of Hougoumont was as vigorously sought for by the enemy, as valiantly defended by the allies; and if victory could have found space for one laurel more, in the thickly-entwined wreath assigned to bravery on that celebrated spot, she would have added it, in honour of the British guards, under the command of the gallant Colonel Hepburn.[2]

Among other most conspicuous instances of corresponding gallantry may be named the repeated brilliant charges of the two regiments of Life-Guards, in which their gallant Colonels Ferrier and Fitzgerald were slain. The matchless conduct of the Royals, the Greys, the Inniskillens, headed by the brave Ponsonby, who yielded up his life in this glorious struggle for Europe's freedom, the intrepid advance against nine thousand of the enemy, of Kempt's brigade, led on by one, whose name is his eulogy, the loved, the chivalrous Picton, who was struck from his horse a lifeless corpse, just as the word "charge" had rung from his lips in a loud and animating tone—the bright example set to the sons of Belgium by the Prince of Orange, from the first opening of the day of strife, until within a short period of its glorious close, when severely wounded, he was carried from the field, where he had so nobly sustained his early frame—these are some of the recollections of Waterloo, that cast a hallowed light over its dark field of carnage; and of such reminiscences, none are of a more lofty character than those inspired by La Haye Sainte. This farm, immediately in front of our left centre, was occupied by five companies of the 2nd light battalion of the German Legion, under Major Baring, and was vigorously assaulted by the enemy. The defenders barely numbered three hundred men, and yet heroically repulsed four desperate attempts of the enemy to gain possession. The walls had been loop-holed for musketry, and from these apertures, as well as from a loft, commanding the road, the marksmen of the Legion committed murderous havoc on the assailants. Officers were the principal objects of their aim, and numbers of these were stretched under the walls by the unerring shots of the Germans. A lull of some minutes usually succeeded the unsuccessful efforts of the enemy to force an entrance, and it was during one of these cessations, that a French cuirassier, for the purpose of ascertaining the real strength of the party within, showed a self-devotion that was very remarkable.

The road to La Belle Alliance passes directly under the walls of La Haye Sainte, and at a distance of about one hundred yards, sinks into a hollow, invisible from the house. The entrance from this road to the garden of La Haye Sainte was defended by an abbatis, constructed of loose timber, and guarded by a detachment of the legion under Lieutenant Græme—a young and gallant Scotchman. The firing had for some time ceased, and the road—as far as it could be seen—was clear, when a French cuirassier was seen upon the ridge of the descent slowly advancing towards the position, round which the dead and dying were thickly strewn.

No aim was taken at him as he approached, for who could guess at the fearless purpose that brought him there? And from the point of his sword being studiously lowered to the earth, during his slow progress forwards, it was supposed he was a deserter. The defenders of the abbatis challenged him as he neared the post; and as no answer was returned, his silence confirmed the supposition that he had deserted from the enemy. As he reached the abbatis, Græme summoned him to surrender; when the bold intruder replied to the demand by quietly raising himself in his stirrups, until he could command an entire view of the party within, and its defences. He then aimed a terrible blow at Græme's head, and turning his horse round, galloped off at lightning speed the way he came. Such was the surprise created by the audacious daring of the man, that although every musket was turned upon him, and he had fully one hundred yards to ride, before he could be screened by the sinking of the road, he escaped in safety to the French lines.

Reduced in number, and with ammunition exhausted, the gallant Germans could maintain themselves no longer in the ruins, to which La Haye Sainte was reduced; and when at length the French infantry, supported by artillery, poured into its walls, the assailants looked round in astonishment at finding barely thirty men to welcome them with their last round of ammunition.[3]

This gallant remnant, that had so nobly obeyed Major Baring's orders to defend the position to the last, was furiously assailed by the enemy; and even the wounded that lay stretched upon the floors, were cruelly bayoneted. The young officer, Græme, whom the chance of war had left uninjured, rushed through the throng of French soldiers, who were glutting their vengeance upon his dying comrades, and miraculously effected his escape through a passage, which led into the open ground upon the right. Perceiving the remainder of his regiment, headed by the gallant Baring, posted behind a stunted hedge at a short distance, he sped towards it through a shower of musketry, and had just reached it, greeted by a shout of welcome from his comrades, when he was struck down with a severe wound.

Thus fell La Haye Sainte, the stout defence of which position, by so inadequate a force, through a long period of the day of strife, reflected on that battalion of the German Legion engaged in its defence—an honour that might well have been commemorated by the name of "La Haye Sainte," appearing in conjunction with that of Waterloo, upon the banners of its regiment.

The softened light of evening had succeeded to the broad glare of day; and how stood the hostile legions that survived the uncompromising advance of time? Still on the one side, flashed the presumptuous daring that attack inspires. Still, on the other, was displayed the same passive submission to a leader's will; but, over both, time had thrown a spell that weighed most heavily on the weaker side; and strong as the spirit still remained, the physical energies of Wellington's soldiers were almost exhausted by protracted endurance of the frightful contest.

The slopes that at morning's dawn had worn their covering of freshest verdure, were at evening's close, heaped depositories of dead men's bodies. The corn that had waved in rich luxuriance, was now trampled to the earth from whence it sprung, staunching with its heavy fruitfulness, many a stream that flowed from the death-gaps of the brave. The clearness of a summer sky was screened by a thick and lurid atmosphere that pressed upon the field of carnage, as gloom presses on the hearts of men, who think themselves sacrificed in vain. And such was, for a time, the thought of many who lived to see the evening hour on the field of Waterloo.

It was nearly seven o'clock, when a thrill of renewed hope and joyful excitement revived the fagged and drooping spirits of our diminished squares and exhausted squadrons. The hour had at length arrived when fortitude and forbearance were to meet with their reward; and as Blucher's guns boomed in the distance, each man felt that the signal of revenge was given in that glad sound. On Napoleon's ear, the echo fell as the knell of departing glory. One hope and one alone remained. The Imperial Guard had never yet been vanquished.

This veteran band of fifteen thousand men, which had taken little part in the contest of the day, was now ordered to charge the British line; and with noble intrepidity, these renowned warriors, headed by the chivalrous Ney, rushed with fresh and unimpaired vigour to our slopes.

As they advanced, a tremendous fire from our artillery poured destruction into their ranks; yet, still pressing forward, they gallantly made their way to the ridge that concealed the British guards. The fate of Europe hung upon the crisis; and fortune held in reserve for Wellington, at that moment, the proudest distinction of his military life.

"Up, guards, and at them," are words that will thrill through the hearts of men, long after who spoke them, and they, who responded to them, are passed away. The guards sprung up from their recumbent position at the welcome command, and poured a volley into the advancing column that stopped effectually its progress. Panic-stricken, the Imperial veterans staggered, as a second well-directed fire took fatal effect among them; and as the British guards charged with overwhelming fury down the hill, these old soldiers durst not meet the shock, but turned and fled in wild disorder, pursued by the victorious guards and Adam's light brigade.

Vainly did some of the *vieille garde*, in reserve at the bottom of the descent, try to reform the routed columns. Our cavalry, headed by the noble Uxbridge, dashed among them, driving them onwards into the thick confusion, that now began to envelope, in every direction, the French army.

By this time, the Prussians were pressing heavily on the right flank of the enemy; and Wellington, no longer restrained by the stern necessity of prudence, which had been so dearly practised throughout the long day of tumult and anxiety, ordered his whole line to advance upon the foe.

The brave allies, forgetting past tribulation in present glory, advanced with loud cheers to the attack; and the last effulgent rays of a setting sun shone on the conqueror, Wellington, as he led the general charge. With desperate valour, the warriors of the Imperial guard endeavoured to check the tide of victory by making a stand worthy of their high repute. Vain effort! Onwards, like a tempestuous torrent rushed the victorious allies, sweeping before them, in one blended mass, a confused and broken multitude, while the Prussian cavalry, animated by a spirit of deadly hatred, followed up the pursuit with eager ferocity, repaying with interest, upon the flying remains of *la grande armée*, their long standing debt of revenge.

On the ground where stood, on the morning of the 18th, this formidable army of Napoleon, the junction of the allies with the

Prussians was consummated at close of day, by the meeting of Wellington and Blucher, and by the mingling together of British and Prussian voices in one heartfelt cry of "victory."

1. Had the squadrons of the cuirassiers been accompanied by a few mounted artillerymen, each provided with some common spikes of four inches in length, and a small hammer—with which the French and English field-batteries are always supplied—they might have been employed during the few moments that the cuirassiers were in possession of our guns, with much advantage to themselves and injury to us.

It would not have occupied the space of half a minute for these artillerymen to have introduced a spike into the vent of a gun, and with a sharp blow from the hammer, to have broken it off flush with the metal—the spike being in cast steel.

This simple operation would have placed our guns *hors de service*, and the result would, in all human probability, have been fatal to the allied army.

2. This officer's name was omitted by the Duke of Wellington—in reference to the defence of Hougoumont—in his Grace's dispatch of the battle of Waterloo, and the name of a junior officer substituted for it. The mistake—which doubtless it was in the first instance—was never rectified, and in consequence every writer upon Waterloo securely firm on the authority of the Duke himself, has failed to render justice to the memory of a gallant officer, and honourable man, by mentioning him as the officer in command on that memorable occasion.

3. It was not owing to the difficulty of communicating with the gallant men, who defended the farm of La Haye Sainte—as it has been asserted—that the failure of their ammunition is to be attributed, but to the exhaustion in the field depôts, of that particular cartridge adapted to the German rifles. Fresh supplies of ammunition had been issued by the Field-Train throughout the entire line, at different periods of the battle, which responsible branch of the service was conducted by the Author of this work. Some regiments expended more than others, and particularly the three battalions of the old 95th; whose calibres differed from the other regiments of the line, and were the same as those of the 2nd light battalion of the Germans. Towards the close of the day, the last round of this species of ammunition had been issued.

There can be no doubt, however, but that La Haye Sainte required for its defence a reinforcement of men, far more than of ammunition. Before the position was taken by the enemy, its defenders were nearly all slain. Ergo, fresh supplies of ammunition would have been of little service to them. Had a battalion of men, and a couple of howitzers been posted within its enclosures, La Haye Sainte would have maintained itself against any assault, as Hougoumont maintained itself, to the close of the day.

CHAPTER XXXII

RETURN TO BRUSSELS

IT was dark when I turned my horse's head in the direction of Brussels, in obedience to orders I had received from Sir George Wood, the commanding officer of artillery, to proceed to that place, and to send forward without a moment's delay, fresh supplies of small arm ammunition for the troops in the field, and the materiel necessary for the re-equipment of the brigades of artillery, after the rough handling they had sustained during the contest.

At a very critical period of the battle, I had brought up to the German batteries, under the gallant Hartmann, the last of the howitzer ammunition that remained in reserve on the field; and it was, therefore, of the first importance that a fresh supply should be obtained with all possible expedition, to replenish the exhausted limber boxes of the guns, as well as the cartouch boxes of the soldiers.

The battle was won, but the sweeping overthrow of the French army by the rapid and indefatigable pursuit of the Prussians was not then known to its full extent; and it was very essential that the thinned ranks of our matchless army should be provided with the means of making a stand worthy of themselves, in the event of the enemy rallying.

The road that led from the field of battle was so densely thronged, that it was a matter of difficulty to thread a narrow pass through the moving crowd. In some places, carts and wagons, filled with dead and dying, stood wedged so tightly together, that many minutes would elapse before they could be disengaged, while the groans of the sufferers within them, the oaths of the drivers, and the entreaties for help from those wounded soldiers who had managed to crawl into ditches for temporary shelter amidst the confusion, combined to create a scene that can never be forgotten by those who witnessed it.

The long straggling street of the village of Waterloo presented a curious appearance. Every house, even to the most lowly, was a blaze of illumination, from the number of candles that flared within, and each window disclosed a crowd of shadowy figures gliding to and fro behind the humble curtains. In those rooms where the wounded lay, might have been seen suffering, in all its sad hues of gloomy colouring, from the young and impetuous soldier—whose leading star had been ambition for distinction, and whose young dream of glory was still lingering on the threshold of memory, even while the cold damps of death were settling upon his brow—to the veteran of many battlefields, in whom age and experience had blotted out those dreams of youth, and whose thoughts, on the bed of death, were turned to the loved home, and desolate hearts of those he left behind.

During the day's engagement, I had seen an officer struck from his horse by a cannon ball, and on going up to him, recognized the gallant Colonel, Sir Alexander Gordon, whom I had known in the Peninsula. Only a few minutes previously I had seen and spoken to Dr. Hume, the head-quarter surgeon; and it was with no small gratification that I assured the poor sufferer that assistance was at hand. By great good fortune, I found Dr. Hume on the spot where I had left him, and his valuable services were quickly afforded to this distinguished officer, who was placed in a blanket, and carried to the rear.

At the village of Waterloo, I inquired with anxiety his fate from an artillery surgeon that I met. Poor fellow! he had just expired, after undergoing amputation of the leg, leaving behind him a bright fame as a soldier and a gentleman.

A little further on, continuing my road, I came up with an artillery cart, in which lay an officer, stretched upon a blanket. My anxiety for many in that gallant corps, caused me to inquire his name, and I learnt with sorrow, deep and true, that young Robert

Manners—the gay, the handsome, the brave—was lying a corpse in that wretched conveyance. I knew that he had lost his leg in the early part of the day; but I little expected to meet him on that dark road, his eye as dark, his joyous voice silenced for ever. I laid my hand upon his breast—it was cold as marble. I pressed his hand, which for the first time, gave no pressure in return, and turned away more sick at heart than words can well express. It was doubly mournful to reflect that this fine fellow might have been saved by remaining where his leg was amputated; but, removed at his own request, too soon after the operation, hemorrhage came on, and his young life ebbed away in that dark, cheerless vehicle, as it jolted over the rough *chaussée* that traverses the gloomy Forest of Soignies.

As I continued my way onwards, the confusion seemed, if possible, to increase. Groups of intoxicated soldiers were congregated on the sides of the roads, adding to the general dismay and alarm, by recklessly firing off their pieces, upon every passing object. Some of the commissariat wagons had been deserted by their drivers; and the empty barrels that rolled upon the road, displayed the means by which liquor had been obtained by the soldiery.

On approaching nearer to Brussels, the inhabitants of that city were thronging forwards to hear tidings from the scene of action—tidings that might be depended on; for so varied and contradictory had been the reports throughout the day, that it was impossible to extract a rational conclusion from so many conflicting falsehoods. The first face I recognized, under the broad glare of a lamp in the Faubourg de la Porte de Namur, was that of Admiral Sir Pulteney Malcolm. The anxiety of his countenance was very great.

"The battle is won. The Duke is safe," were my first words.

"God be praised for both," said the veteran sailor, with an "onction" that could not have been surpassed by his holiness, the Pope; and at the moment, I really believe that we could, though we did not, have hugged each other, *à la française*, for joy. Sir Pulteney Malcolm had been sent by the Admiralty to Ostend, to be in readiness for any emergency that might require his aid. Like a true British blue jacket, he could not endure being kept so far from the scene of action; therefore, leaving his ship, he came to Brussels to obtain the earliest information of what was going on. Having heard my news, the Admiral started off again, with the same zealous impatience to be the first to announce the great victory of Waterloo to his gallant crew.

My jaded horse dragged his weary legs, at a slow pace, through the crowded streets of Brussels, seeming little to participate in the triumphant feelings that were beginning to assume a decided ascendancy. Had victory been on the side of the French, it is probable that the demonstrations of joy evinced by the populace, at the success of the allies, would have been equally vehement, and more sincere. The events that have since occurred in Belgium justify such an opinion, by proving how ready she would have been to incorporate herself with France, had Europe so consented. But leaving that as an uncertainty, it will be admitted by all, that greater enthusiasm could not have been displayed, than when tidings of the victory of Waterloo were received. Nor in the annals of war were the inhabitants of Brussels ever surpassed in the humanity and tenderness they exhibited towards the distressed wounded of all nations, that assisted in the glorious result.

At that late hour, women of the highest rank were hastening to the hospitals, with lint and necessaries for the sufferers. Some even took upon themselves to assist the surgeons in their painful duties, and watched with gentle assiduity by the pallets of the wounded soldiers, throughout that long night of agony to so many. Each hour added to the noise and confusion of the town. The arrival of vehicles of every description, bringing in the wounded from the scene of the day's battle, appeared endless; and the cheers of the mob, as our soldiers came galloping in, with some proud trophy of the victory, mingled in strange discordance with the laments of women seeking among the wounded, their relatives and friends.

After having communicated with the field-train officer, in charge at Brussels, upon the object of my mission, I retired to my quarters; but sleep, I can well believe, visited the eyelids of few, who returned that night from the field of Waterloo. Time seemed to have made a leap that placed a chasm between the events that had occurred before the opening of the battle, and those that had since happened, leaving memory in possession only of the latter. It was impossible to believe that the day which was past, and the night which was passing, were limited, by the hand of time, to so short a space; for within the first, an eternity of feeling had been concentrated, which the latter was reflecting with a shadowy, but painful accuracy, and the shouts of men, the clang of arms, and battle's thunder, that had prolonged the day to an immeasurable length, were scarcely more exciting in their reality than was the repetition of them, by a fatigued imagination, throughout the night.

Such sensations did not fall to my share alone. I have heard others describe the turbulence of their dreams on the night of the 18th of June, 1815; but, when another rising sun dawned upon the world, it brought with it an invigorated healthfulness to the mind; and exultation, and joyful gratitude, that victory had again crowned her favoured Wellington in the great cause of freedom on the field of Waterloo.

CHAPTER XXXIII

A FINAL ADVENTURE

THE tempest which had threatened the world was hushed, and the dawn of a lasting peace seemed to have risen from its scattered elements. France, with apparent sincerity, called upon her legitimate Ruler to resume his position, and he, in turn, admitted past error, and promised that experience should be his guide for the future.[1] The army still adhered with faithful tenacity, to the name of Napoleon, and even after an abdication, which resembled the mock-heroic *denouement* of a stage performance, a host of gallant men held together, under the banner of the tricolore. The towns and fortresses of France were garrisoned by these troops, and while Wellington and Blucher pursued their victorious route towards the capital, levelling whatever obstructions impeded their progress, the second corps of the Prussian army, under the command of Prince Augustus of Prussia, was directed to reduce the northern frontier fortresses of Maubeuge, Landrecy, Philippeville, Marienbourg, and Rocroy; a powerful and well-equipped battering train—to the charge of which I was appointed—having been placed by Wellington at the disposal of the Prussian Prince, to effect these operations.[2]

The frontier fortresses were all well garrisoned, and in a good state of defence. Philippeville and Landrecy had received reinforcements in the fugitives from Waterloo, and the gallant stand they made against the formidable armament brought to reduce them, shewed the fidelity of the French soldiers to their flag, even after it had ceased to represent the power of the extraordinary man who had adopted it as his own. Yet it is just to the Commandants of these fortresses to observe, that they were not desirous of an unnecessary effusion of blood, for when summoned in succession to surrender, by Prince Augustus, each replied, that he was ready to open the gates intrusted to his keeping, upon receiving orders to that effect, from whatever government existed, at the time being, in Paris. No such orders were given, nor indeed was sufficient time allowed for receiving them; and consequently the fortresses were consigned to the unnecessary horrors of bombardment, which was the mode of attack adopted by the Prussians, to the great injury of the inhabitants and houses, especially at Philippeville, where conflagration destroyed nearly half the town.

Each fortress was taken in succession: Maubeuge was the first attacked, and held out five days. Landrecy was the next, and was reduced after a period of two days. Phiippeville suffered severely from the town being bombarded and set on fire in many places, and surrendered on the fourth day. Marienbourg capitulated after a bombardment of three days, and lastly Rocroy, which made a stout resistance of five days.

After the capitulation of each fortress, the garrison marched out with the honours of war, dispersing immediately in every direction, with a celerity that was marvellous. Not a French soldier tarried behind to witness the ingenious method adopted by the Prussians to maintain an army at little cost, or rather to ensure to themselves a remuneration for the trouble of coming so far from home, to return the visit made by the French to them in Prussia.

The first step taken by the Prince, on entering the captured town, was to call upon the civil authorities to provide quarters for himself and staff, suitable billets for the Generals and other officers, and billets and rations for the troops, on a scale of quantity and quality designated by himself; exacting also that the best provisions and wine should be supplied at the same economical ratio, to every officer, Prussian and British, who accompanied him.[3] Nor was this all. These snug little towns contained hoards very precious to the army, of cloth, linen, and leather. A strong hand was laid upon them also; and it was required of the inhabitants, that not only these articles should be appropriated to the wants of the troops, but that all the tailors, sempstresses, and shoemakers that the town could muster, should be employed day and night to replace, by their handicraft, the wear and tear occasioned by the long marches that were necessary to bring the Prussians to these forest fastnesses.

The pursuance of this course was considered by Prince Augustus as perfectly justifiable, when carrying on war in an enemy's country, repressing on one side all excesses and cruelty in the troops under his command, and exacting, on the other, that they should be supplied with every necessary they stood in need of; and when the blood-stained route of the French army through Prussia is remembered, the moderate and equitable demands made on the inhabitants of the French towns, on this occasion, stand forth in honourable contrast.

The discipline of the Prussian troops during this short campaign was admirably maintained, and displayed to advantage the qualities of the Prussian soldier, which are—high courage, an exalted love of country, patience under privation, and devotion to his officers, who are, in themselves, well worthy to inspire a feeling that tends very materially to the high organization of the Prussian army.

On the morning that preceded the capitulation of Rocroy, I was returning from a mortar battery to the park of artillery, to forward fresh supplies of ammunition, when perplexed by the many cross roads that intersect the forest of the Ardennes, I chanced, most inopportunely, to take one that led me to a French piquet. The surprize of the French soldiers at the appearance of an English officer among them was great; but my chagrin was greater still at being taken prisoner at that eleventh hour. Chagrin and regrets were, however, alike unavailing, and I was marched off into the fortress, with many a *mauvaise plaisanterie* to beguile me on the way. The interior of the garrison shewed the feelings of the French military at that moment. The capitulation of this last fortress, on whose walls still proudly waved the tricolore, was hourly expected, and the excitement of the soldiers, at the necessity of surrendering to the Prussians the banner under which they had fought and conquered at Jena, amounted to savage frenzy.

My reception, as I passed through a crowd of half drunken soldiers, was none of the most friendly. Execrations on England and the English greeted me on every side, and it was only when I found myself in the presence of the Commandant that I considered my life in security from the inflamed passions of the soldiery. At an early hour, the officers of the garrison sat down to dinner, and I was invited to join this meeting, that was looked upon as the last, in which they were to be assembled in the brotherhood of arms. The turbulence of that party can only find an excuse in the conflicting feelings that waged fiercely in the breasts of men, peculiarly susceptible by their national character, to the humiliation of defeat. The room was crowded beyond what it could hold with any degree of ease, and wine flowed with a freeness that soon took effect upon imaginations already over-heated.

The drinkers, from enthusiastic, became literally mad, and shouts and oaths, mingled in one furious uproar with uncorking of bottles, and smashing of glasses against each other, to the health of the Emperor Napoleon. Spurred on by the uncontrollable frenzy of the moment, the Commandant turned suddenly and fiercely upon me, insisting that I should drink to "*L'Empereur.*" I declined the honour, as in duty bound, when this *officier supérieur*, no longer able to withstand the dictates of hatred that were urging him on to wreak his vengeance on an Englishman arose, and with his sword unsheathed, swore with a tremendous "*Sacré nom de Dieu,*" that I should not leave the table until I had complied with his demand.

If it be true that "*in vino veritas,*" the French character was nobly redeemed by what followed. A simultaneous rush was made towards me by a phalanx of brave fellows, whose countenances spoke eloquently their indignation at conduct so unchivalrous and ungenerous towards a prisoner. Nor was their example lost upon the aggressor, for throwing his hostile weapon at a distance from him, he rushed to embrace me, at the risk of excoriating the sides of my face with a stubble beard of at least a ten days' growth. The remainder of the day was passed in riot and uproar, and on the following morning terms of capitulation were sent in by the Commandant to Prince Augustus.

That morning was one of proud and yet painful feelings. Seated on his beautiful charger, Prince Augustus surveyed his well-dressed, well-disciplined troops, as they marched past him, their fine bands playing the martial airs, of their liberated country, while the triumph of conquest imparted a proud confidence, which was perceptible in their whole appearance. The last sound of the cannon had been heard which had revenged the wrongs of Prussia; and as memory retraced those wrongs, and with them the sorrows and humiliations to which Prussia's beautiful and high-minded Queen had been exposed, a sigh of regret arose that she had not been spared, to witness the regeneration of the land she so dearly loved.

Such was the picture presented by the Prussian troops, as they filed past their Prince; nor was it less interesting to behold the garrison of Rocroy, as with defiance still marked upon their faces, the veterans marched out with the honours of war, and piled the arms that had so often been victorious, upon the glacis of the fortress. How was it possible not to think of Friedland, Austerlitz, and Wagram, on seeing the groups that now congregated together to take a last farewell. Distinctions of rank had been cast off with the arms they bore, and officers wept, and grasped the extended hands of privates, with the affection that men feel, who have been bound together by the tie of mutual danger, and the comradeship of military life.

As soon as the French garrison had dispersed, Prince Augustus made known his wish of taking leave of those British officers who had taken part in the recent campaign.

Dismounting from his horse, and surrounded by his staff, his Royal Highness placed himself on the ramparts of the fortress, on which the Prussian Eagle now floated in the breeze, and addressing us in English, he dwelt with noble enthusiasm, on the restoration of liberty to nations, and peace to Europe, through the instrumentality—in a great degree—of England and of Prussia. He spoke of the curse of war, as too dearly proved by years of insolent aggression on the part of France; and gave it, as his firm belief, that Germany—integral Germany, the heart of Europe—undivided in her policy, and united to England by the adamantine chain of mutual confidence, might defy all future efforts to disturb her peace.

The Prince then returned us, individually, his thanks for our services; and as a mixed group of Prussian and British officers stood on the glacis of Rocroy, exchanging heartfelt assurances of kindly feeling, and regret at parting, each felt an honest pride at having contributed his share to the conclusion of a war, that in ages yet to come, will shine among the most glorious in the page of History.

1. Vide Louis XVIII's proclamation to the French nation, dated Cambray, June 28, 1815.

2. On the morning that succeeded the battle of Waterloo, the author was specially appointed to the charge of the battering-train, placed at the disposal of the Prussian army, for the reduction of the French frontier fortresses. This battering-train, which was on a scale of extraordinary magnitude, consisted of two hundred and forty-five heavy guns and mortars; two hundred and eighty-eight thousand rounds of shot and shells; nineteen thousand barrels of gunpowder, with a pontoon train, and other heavy stores. From this immense park of artillery, which had been collected and equipped for service at Brussels, seventy-five heavy guns and mortars were transported over cross roads, measuring a distance of two hundred and ninety miles to the scenes of warfare. Three thousand horses of the country were required to move this ponderous train from one point of attack to another.

Six companies of British artillery accompanied this expedition under the command of Sir Alexander Dickson.

3. After the capture of Marienbourg, Prince Augustus issued orders for the defences of the town to be destroyed, and directed that the inhabitants should furnish the working parties for the purpose.

On the same day, Sir Alexander Dickson and myself dined with the Prince in the fortress, when His Royal Highness jocosely asked me, what I thought of his method of making war. I answered that I had every reason to consider it the best method I had yet witnessed. "Comment cela," said the Prince, "you have served under Wellington in the Peninsula and at Waterloo." "True, your Royal Highness; but in those countries

I was obliged to spend my money, and here I keep it, and am much better lodged and fed into the bargain." "Ah!" said the Prince, laughing, "L'Angleterre est plus riche que la Prusse, et plus généreuse aussi."

There was a sly sarcasm in his manner, that lent an interpretation to his words, as the moral does to the fable.

THE END

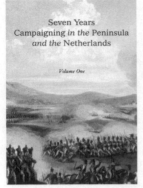

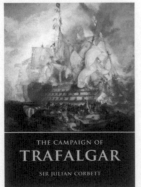